I0112620

Praise for

VENTURE MODE

"Business schools are failing students. They focus on administration, HR, accounting, and cost. They portray value as something managers magically add, like a markup on a widget. And they produce graduates mired in stale bureaucratic thinking. *Venture Mode* is the antidote. As its capable authors make clear, business needs more value creators and fewer managers. Value is not the mysterious byproduct of rigid processes—it's the starting point and critical focus. Smart businesses relentlessly seek to understand the consumer's experience and work backward. The book lays out the critical principles every business needs to move away from bureaucracy and toward value creation. It's an eye-opening expose of what's wrong with the MBA factories. It's a clarion call for a new way of thinking about business. More than anything, *Venture Mode* is the mindset shift every entrepreneur needs for the twenty-first century."

JEFF DEIST, general counsel, Monetary Metals & Co.; former president, Mises Institute

"*Venture Mode* offers an entrepreneurial approach to business education that applies intense focus to customer needs, empathetic innovation, subjective value, entrepreneurial action, and networks. Its original perspective highlights how traditional thinking has ill-equipped leaders for today's dynamic markets, where value creation drives thriving. By demanding an educational approach that nurtures empathy, ingenuity, judgment, and tenacity, business schools can help unleash entrepreneurial leaders.

"*Venture Mode* offers three novel elements to the ongoing rethinking of management:

1. Education based on providing a true understanding of the drivers of innovative value creation and generative market shifts.
2. Experiential learning rather than classrooms and textbooks.
3. A business model in which the hiring party is the customer.

"*Venture Mode* is a revolutionary alternative to current models of business education, rooted in the entrepreneurial pursuit of new value creation."

STEPHEN DENNING, former World Bank executive, *Forbes* senior contributor, and author of *The Age of Agile*

"*Venture Mode* is a striking rethink of business education brimming with creative insight. Hunter Hastings and Mark Packard reveal how "administrative mode" has suffocated innovation. Their proposal is fresh, entrepreneurial, and rooted in value creation. The authors' thoughtful framework transforms how we think about leadership and learning. The book provides a blueprint for the future of business . . . so needed for today's dynamic markets."

DENNIS LOPEZ, CEO, Global Real Estate Company

"The MBA may be the gold standard in business credentials—but is it gold-plated nonsense? In *Venture Mode*, Hastings and Packard argue it's not just overrated—it's counterproductive. The problem lies in the 'A' for administration, which suffocates the 'B' for business. Instead of fostering value creation and customer focus, the MBA mindset breeds bureaucracy, control, and rigid routines. Managers are trained like battlefield generals, not builders of innovation. Business schools teach command and compliance, not creativity. What's lost? The entrepreneur—the true engine of the market—who thrives by serving, not scheming."

PER BYLUND, PhD, associate professor of entrepreneurship and Johnny D. Pope Chair, Spears School of Business, Oklahoma State University

"I spent a lifetime researching how firms create long-term value, establishing that a knowledge-building culture is the key determinant of long-term performance. In contrast, the most popular theory of the firm in business schools is agency theory that focuses on ways to control the adversarial relationships between principals and agents. Hastings and Packard unpack the evolution of business school education to plainly reveal the dominance of control, i.e., administration (the 'A' in MBA), that guides the MBA curriculum and also to explain why we need a new alternative. My work is complementary to Hastings and Packard, with their game plan for escaping the administration trap. *Venture Mode* lays the foundation for a needed paradigm change for business school education, beginning with the goal to better understand the value-creation process in order to significantly improve our performance as value creators in our business careers. In reading the book's ten chapters, I was struck by the implications of this new paradigm for living the good life. That is, living one's life to create value for others, and in so doing, create value for yourself—earned success."

BARTLEY J. MADDEN, former managing director, Credit Suisse HOLT, and author of *Value Creation Insights: A Foundational Understanding of How Firms Build Knowledge and Create Value*

"*Venture Mode* is a manifesto that redefines business success for the AI age. By contrasting the stifling constraints of traditional administration mode with the dynamic freedom of what they call 'venture mode,' the authors illuminate a path to unprecedented adaptability and innovative success. This book harnesses entrepreneurial economics to nurture creativity, turning rigid planning into fluid experimentation and feedback-driven growth. In an era dominated by AI, these venture mode skills are no longer optional—they are essential life skills for thriving amid constant change. The proposed Masters of Business Enterprise (MBE) revolutionizes curriculum, business models, and experiential learning, empowering corporations as true stakeholders. A must-read for anyone ready to unleash entrepreneurial potential and help build a thriving new economy. This visionary work will inspire leaders to embrace change and drive transformative progress."

CURTIS R. CARLSON, PhD, professor of practice, Northeastern University; former CEO, SRI International in Silicon Valley

HUNTER HASTINGS
AND MARK PACKARD

VENTURE MODE

Escape the Administration Trap by Finding and Unleashing Entrepreneurial Leaders

www.amplifypublishinggroup.com

Venture Mode: Escape the Administration Trap by Finding and Unleashing Entrepreneurial Leaders

For more information, please contact:
Amplify Publishing, an imprint of Amplify Publishing Group
620 Herndon Parkway, Suite 220
Herndon, VA 20170
info@amplifypublishing.com

Library of Congress Control Number: 2025924373

CPSIA Code: PRV1125A

ISBN-13: 979-8-89138-651-8

Printed in the United States

VENTURE MODE

Venture mode is a bold shift in business management, taking the creative entrepreneurial economics behind successful start-ups and high-growth firms and unleashing it for all businesses. Venture mode starts from imagining the value that end users crave, creates innovative new pathways to deliver that value, and obsesses relentlessly over customer feedback to keep refining value at high speed.

Venture mode ditches the MBA's fixation on hierarchy, bureaucracy, control, and continuity. It slices through dead weight, slashing anything that doesn't serve the end user, to drive business effectiveness and killer returns. It's the antidote to stagnation, built for energetic innovators eager to transform their businesses into value-creating powerhouses.

CONTENTS

PART III: THE FUTURE

FOREWORD

As an organizational consultant with a passion for dismantling bureaucracy and fostering self-management, I am thrilled to endorse *Venture Mode* by Hunter Hastings and Mark Packard. This book is a clarion call for a revolution in business education and practice, exposing the deep flaws of the "administration mode" that dominates traditional business schools and corporate structures. The authors' incisive critique resonates deeply with my advocacy for thriving self-managed organizations. *Venture Mode* articulates a bold vision for unleashing entrepreneurial leaders who prioritize customer value, empathy, and innovation over control and metrics—a paradigm shift that aligns perfectly with the future of work.

Hastings and Packard brilliantly dissect how the MBA-driven focus on bureaucracy, rooted in scientific management, produces administrators rather than innovators, stifling the entrepreneurial spirit essential for today's dynamic markets. Their evidence, from founder-led successes like Tesla to the stagnation of metric-obsessed firms, is compelling. The book's thesis—that business education is killing business by churning out leaders ill-equipped for value creation—hits hard and true. As someone who has seen organizations bogged down by hierarchies and red tape, I find their call to "blow up the business school" both urgent and inspiring.

The introduction of "venture mode" as an alternative is a game-changer. The authors' ten key points, particularly the emphasis on customer sovereignty, empathy as a critical skill, and networks over hierarchies, mirror my own principles of self-organization. Their focus on qualitative value—emotional attachment and trust—over quantitative obsession is a refreshing antidote to the financialization that plagues administration mode. The principles of venture mode, from busting bureaucracy to prioritizing action over rigid strategy, offer a practical road map for organizations seeking agility and purpose. I sense echoes of my own work in their advocacy for permissionless innovation and self-managing teams.

The proposed Master of Business Enterprise (MBE) is a visionary reimagining of education, aligned with experiential and value-driven learning. By positioning hiring corporations as customers who invest in ready-to-innovate talent, Hastings and Packard propose a model that could transform how we prepare leaders. Their emphasis on entrepreneurial economics and apprenticeship-like modalities challenges the status quo and offers a path to nurture ingenuity and tenacity.

Venture Mode is a must-read for executives, consultants, and academics ready to break free from the administration trap. It's a blueprint for cultivating leaders who can navigate complexity with empathy and action, ensuring businesses thrive in a value-driven economy. This book doesn't just diagnose the problem—it provides a revolutionary solution. I wholeheartedly recommend it to anyone committed to redefining leadership for the modern world.

DOUG KIRKPATRICK

Organizational consultant and author of *Beyond Empowerment: The Age of the Self-Managed Organization* and *The No-Limits Enterprise: Organizational Self-Management in the New World of Work*

PREFACE

The world is full of administrators. Just listen and observe: From politicians to leaders in business, academia, and other sectors, nearly all pursue effective administration. The world's top leaders are praised or criticized for their selection of members of their administration, and these administrators then go on to employ an army of bureaucrats to enact their administrative tasks.

Business and organization leaders are praised for their administrative skills, which are the focus of countless tomes on effective leadership. And those who seek to become business leaders one day will often pursue formal training in administration, offered in business schools around the world. The peak of this academic training is the master of business administration—the MBA.

This book, however, is a call for radical reform. And the error we hope to root out is *administration*. The world right now needs more entrepreneurs and fewer administrators.

Administration, if it has any role at all, belongs buried within the deeper levels of organizations, where it should remain unseen and can do little harm. In fact, most businesses don't need it at all and would do far better with only entrepreneurial leaders—the antithesis of administrators—instead.

Yet, most modern businesses are almost fully staffed with trained administrators, from top to bottom. Top leaders often become obsessive administrators, persistently seeking greater operational efficiency and continuous improvements in metrics. It's not their fault, really. That's what they're taught to believe and do. It's what wins in the short term. But in the long term, administration is always and ultimately disastrous.

Underneath this persistent but archaic mode of business operations is an education system that is itself fundamentally rooted in administration. It's run by administrators for administrators, protecting its bureaucracy from entrepreneurial disruption. And the education that it produces is fundamentally administrative. As a consequence, universities continue to create a bursting supply pipeline of new administrators versus a mere trickle of entrepreneurs.

This rampant administration is strangling the world's entrepreneurial spirit. In a 2013 study,[1] economists John Dawson and John Seater estimated that the total cost of the federal bureaucracy and its ever-mounting administrative regulations to economic growth has been 2 percentage points per year. "Our estimates," they wrote in the *Journal of Economic Growth*, "indicate that annual output by 2005 is about 28% of what it would have been had regulation remained at its 1949 level."[2]

What this means, as Ronald Bailey put it in 2013, is that "the average American household receives about $277,000 less annually than it would have gotten in the absence of six decades of accumulated regulations—a median household income of $330,000 instead of the

$53,000 we get now."[3] Over a decade later, the median income has increased to over $80,000, increasing the estimated cost of administrative regulations to our lives today to about $418,000 annually.

In another study published in 2017 in the *Journal of Regulatory Economics*, economists James Bailey and Diana Thomas found strong evidence that regulations impede entrepreneurship. "Our results," they write, "suggest that from 1998 to 2011, increased federal regulation reduced the entry of new firms by 1.2% and reduced hiring by 2.2%. That result implies that returning to the level of regulation in effect in 1998 would lead to the creation of 30 new firms and the hiring of 530 new employees every year for an average industry."[4]

Administrators are strangling our businesses and economy.

But even this estimate grossly underappreciates the problem because what it doesn't (and can't) account for are all the *new* industries that never came to be—economist Per Bylund calls this "the unrealized."[5] What's more, it's difficult or perhaps impossible to estimate the total *underperformance* of businesses led by administrators rather than entrepreneurs.

In this book we'll attempt to lay the problem bare and at the feet of administration. Most businesses are run in what we will call *administration mode*. We'll then outline the solution—entrepreneurial leadership—which runs a business in what we call *venture mode*. We'll unpack the principles of venture mode, which those who are deeply trained in administration will likely find counterintuitive. But entrepreneurial leaders—those who already run their business(es) in venture mode—will find in this book not only validation of their approach but also a deep, theory-based explanation of the philosophy of entrepreneurial leadership.

We'll then point the finger at modern education—and especially the MBA—as the primary culprit in instilling principles of administration rather than of entrepreneurship. Business school leaders and faculty may balk at this claim, since they (nearly) all teach entrepreneurship. (Sometimes, an introductory entrepreneurship course is even *required* in business schools.) But the deep irony is that they teach entrepreneurship in administration mode, as we will show.

Finally, we will propose some solutions for entrepreneurs to consider and, perhaps, take on. Our primary solution is what we are calling the *MBE*—a master in business *enterprise*. This alternative curriculum and credential would instill the principles of entrepreneurial leadership, as we'll explain them.

WHERE DID THIS BOOK COME FROM?

Hunter, Mark, and a few others began a project a few years back to translate "Austrian" or entrepreneurial economics—which is considered heterodox in the academy—into practical business lessons. We launched a twelve-module minicourse—the *Value Creators*—which is chock-full of powerful insights that you won't learn pretty much anywhere else. We soon realized that what we were developing was much bigger.

After a few evolutionary pivots, we turned our creative minds toward disrupting higher education. We've learned, so far, that higher education is a tough industry to disrupt. It's highly entrenched and protected, not only by academic collectives like the accreditation agencies but also by the world's governments.

For some reason, most people believe that education should be shielded from entrepreneurial disruption. It's a strange sentiment. It's virtually unheard of in other industries, where jobs are rarely protected from entrepreneurial disruption. Perhaps this is the reason why most other industries have demonstrated improving quality and declining costs over time, while the costs of education (along with the medical industries) have skyrocketed with declining quality over time.

This book was, in large part, inspired by our efforts. We wondered if we might get more traction—change people's minds about the promise of entrepreneurship in education—through persuasion.

The core and titular concept of the book—*venture mode*—was inspired by Airbnb cofounder and CEO, Brian Chesky, (and Y Combinator founder Paul Graham) who recently introduced the world to the concept of *founder mode*. Chesky discovered the problem with administration and started to put his finger on a solution. *Bravo!*

But while we agree with a lot of what Chesky has learned, *founder mode* isn't quite right. So this book is an effort to more clearly explain and expound what the problem really is (administration) and what a real solution to it (entrepreneurial leadership) looks like.

The problem is administration, and the solution is *venture mode*.

PART I

THE PAST

CHAPTER 1

BLOWING UP THE BUSINESS SCHOOL

The business school is killing business. This is an odd claim from an authorship team that includes a business professor.[1] But we're convinced it's true. Why? Because it teaches business *administration*, which is the worst way to run a business.

Worldwide, about a quarter of a million people enroll in a master of business administration (MBA) program each year, almost two-thirds of them in the United States. The MBA is a common next step for aspiring employees, a rung upward on the corporate ladder. Many employers will even pay the tuition, in whole or in part, for this education, often in exchange for a certain commitment to the company.

The incentives to obtain the degree are easy enough to identify. MBAs have higher average salaries and are more likely to get higher-level management positions. Job opportunities increase, as many positions will require the credential. But an MBA isn't necessary for business leadership, and it doesn't seem to help in business success.

Elon Musk didn't get an MBA, nor did Jeff Bezos, Marc Andreessen, or eighty-five of the one hundred billionaires on the Forbes 2020 list.[2]

So what's the value of the MBA to a *business*, or more broadly, to the *economy*? The evidence suggests *not much at all*. In fact, it may even be harmful to business and the economy. We might counterfactually be better off had we all just skipped college.

But isn't there plenty of evidence that going to college corresponds to higher future earnings? Absolutely. But this evidence doesn't really demonstrate that it's the *education* that makes the difference, as is widely believed. All it really demonstrates is that people who are more likely to succeed are more likely to go to college first. Because that's what we're expected to do.

For example, *where* you get the degree matters a great deal with respect to future earnings, not because it's a better education, but because it signals a certain level of competence—the education itself is virtually the same everywhere. Why do the smartest students pay tens of thousands more to go to an Ivy rather than a smaller (and much cheaper) school, despite their using the same textbooks and cases and teaching the same skills, tools, and information? They do it because high-paying companies would rather hire from Harvard or Wharton than from Bo Diddley Business School. Those companies have higher confidence that the Ivy students are smart and capable. Studies have found that there's actually almost no *educational* value in higher ed.[3]

But our argument goes beyond the claim that the MBA is just a credential. We're saying that the way MBA students are trained and educated results in *poorer* business performance. They're not trained in the modern, entrepreneurial business approach that produces innovation, growth, and new value for customers. Instead, they're trained in *administration*.

BUSINESS ADMINISTRATION IS THE PROBLEM

Business administration, as it's taught in business schools and enshrined in the MBA degree, is a costly category error. We roughly estimate that it has cost the US 50 percent of its productivity potential.[4] MBA recipients move into or advance within the field of business, where they inappropriately apply the concepts of control and prediction that they learned in school in the form of the tools of "administration" (or, more often, "management"). Although an MBA degree is a generally valid signal of individual intelligence and capabilities, the training provided by MBA programs effectively constrains the creativity, agility, and adaptive economic value creation activities called for in today's economy. The MBA teaches its students how to operate the machinery of corporate control, limiting a firm's possibility space just at the time when this space needs to be expanded for the opportunities of the new digital age.

The modern business administration degree is aptly named—born out of the "scientific management" paradigm[5] that promised ultimate, science-based business efficiency and technocracy. The current MBA curriculum constitutes cut-and-paste analyses, decision frameworks, and operational guidelines that many organizations have consequently followed for decades. The result too often has been the centralization of management power and authority among the MBA educated, who have imposed bureaucratic processes and rigidly standardized practices, governed by heavy-handed control mechanisms and the quantification of outputs ("make the numbers"). They have inadvertently suppressed the entrepreneurial mindset and ethic, composed of empathic value creation, experiential quality, and a focus on individual well-being.

Business administration is anti-entrepreneurial. It rejects the centrally human aspects of business in favor of statistical enumeration and maximization analysis, resulting in large-scale disengagement on the part of employees[6] and deep skepticism of business motivations on the part of consumers and society at large. Whatever customer value is created is increasingly extracted for the narrow financial interests of a sliver of institutionalized investors and stock traders.

The consequences have been disastrous, although the abysmal performance of the MBA-led corporation has long been concealed by the fact that *most* large organizations have been led by the same MBA-wielding administrators who have followed the same prescriptive playbook. Only recently have the real consequences of this bureaucratic administration style of management been more clearly manifested. In recent years, administrative firms have been utterly and undeniably outclassed by their more entrepreneurial counterparts—particularly those who kept their founders through the scaling process rather than replace them with MBA graduates, as has been the conventional wisdom.

FOUNDER MODE

At a Y Combinator event in late August 2024, Airbnb cofounder and CEO, Brian Chesky, gave a talk that instantly changed the conversation in Silicon Valley and the business world more broadly. Paul Graham spread the word in a widely read blog post.[7]

In the talk, Chesky explained that traditional wisdom holds that founders don't have the administrative know-how to manage the scaling up of their venture. Therefore, it is standard practice to bring in an experienced administrator after a successful launch to take the venture to the next level. Graham captured this proposition as two different ways or "modes" of running a company: *founder mode* and *manager mode*. After a good launch, the start-up should switch from founder mode to manager mode, handing the reins over to experienced administrators who can effectively manage the scaling process.

Chesky put into words the mounting sense among industry leaders and venture capitalists that there is something wrong with the conventional wisdom of how ventures transition to large-scale organizations by turning to professional administration. Hired executives too often fail to achieve what they're brought in for, while founders who stay in charge of their start-up have proven to have the higher success rate.

A few examples are in order.

Nest's Tony Fadell

Tony Fadell is the quintessential tech entrepreneur. After a stint at Philips Electronics, he started his own company, Fuse, to develop consumer electronics, including a small, hard disk–based music player and online store for music. Apple scooped him up, where he turned his concept into the initial design for the iPod. In fact, he's often called the "father of the iPod."[8] He and his team created the first eighteen generations of the iPod, as well as the first three generations of the iPhone.

Fadell's next act was equally visionary: He left Apple to cofound Nest Labs in 2010. Nest brought radical design and user-experience thinking to home devices, starting with its smart thermostat—a category that barely existed at the time. Fadell's design-first, user-focused vision was central to Nest's success and appeal.

In 2014, Google acquired Nest and folded it into their broader hardware division. Over time, Fadell clashed with Google executives over the integration of Nest's culture and creative approach into Google's more administrative and data-driven structure. The administrative logic of optimization incrementally replaced Nest's logic of creativity. Product risk gave way to process discipline, and design decisions became committee decisions. Frustrated by the increasing bureaucracy, dilution of design priorities, and a shift from bold innovation to business caution, Fadell left Nest in 2016.

Fadell's story illustrates the problem of the administrative mindset: A creative, visionary founder—eccentric by traditional business standards—becomes marginalized once the firm is absorbed into a system run by MBA-wielding administrators who prioritize predictability, process, and scale over innovation, boldness, and founder instinct. He has since spoken explicitly about how traditional corporate logic smothers innovation:

> Most big companies today are run by people with MBAs. They're not product people. They're process people.[9]

The MBA-trained executive often excels at reducing variability and improving efficiency. But founders like Fadell don't begin with process. They begin with user dissatisfaction—Fadell calls it a "pain point"—and the belief that something in the world is missing or broken, and they try to fix it by creating something radically new. This entrepreneurial approach is often viewed as threatening to "business as usual." Visionary founders are seen as rogues by the professional managerial class, incompatible with the operating system of a "well-managed" company.

Apple and Steve Jobs

An even more familiar example is that of Steve Jobs, who was ousted twice from leadership at Apple because of his perceived weaknesses in business administration—first in 1977 and then again in 1985. The first time, Jobs and cofounder Steve Wozniak had just introduced the Apple II, and early Apple investor Mike Markkula decided to recruit Mike Scott, or "Scotty," who had been director of manufacturing at National Semiconductor, to run the show since the Steves were so young and inexperienced.

Jobs still held primary equity, and when Apple went public, he was appointed chairman of the board. Scotty was eventually pushed aside and replaced by Markkula in 1981, and in 1983, Jobs lured John Sculley, a fifteen-year executive at a Fortune 100 company, PepsiCo, to step into the Apple CEO role.

Meanwhile, Jobs was running the Macintosh project. Known for a notoriously short temper, Jobs rubbed many people the wrong way—within the company *and* on the board. Jobs and Sculley in particular had strong strategic disagreements. But with the generally poor performance of the Macintosh at the time (particularly relative to main competitor IBM), the board ultimately sided with Sculley, and Jobs was ousted in 1985.

Immediately, Jobs set out to start a new company, NeXT Computer. A year later, he also funded a spinout from Lucasfilm that would become Pixar. Meanwhile, Apple gained some traction with the Macintosh, but the PC and its low-cost "clones" running Microsoft Windows started to take over the market in the 1990s. Apple struggled to keep pace.

NeXT, however, did well enough that it was eventually acquired in 1997 by the waffling Apple. The acquisition also facilitated the return of Jobs to be the head of Apple. Readers will know the rest, as Jobs quickly turned Apple around and led it to become the most successful company in the world.

Zynga and Mark Pincus

Another interesting example of this phenomenon is social video game developer Zynga, founded in 2007 by Mark Pincus. Pincus is an interesting character—by all accounts a very bright mind, but he freely admits that he "got fired or [was] asked to leave from all [his] jobs."[10] He apparently just wasn't cut out to work for others, although he teaches prospective entrepreneurs that it's much better to learn how to do business with someone else's money on the line.

By the time he started Zynga at the age of forty-one, Pincus had already launched and sold three other companies. He was one of the pioneers of Web 1.0, launching the first web-based push company, FreeLoader, with a loan of $250,000, which he sold after a mere seven months for $38 million. He was also an early investor in Napster, Facebook, and Twitter, among many others.

Almost everything he touched turned to gold. But not quite.

He started a tech incubator in 2000, just in time for the dot-com crash. And in 2005, he was ousted from Tribe.net—one of the first social networks, which he started in 2003. He bought it back the next year when it almost ran out of cash and then sold its technology to Cisco in 2007 for an undisclosed amount. Another failure was Tag Sense, an online ad venture that didn't last long.

But these successes and failures led Pincus into the social media space, and he became very aware of and involved in its development. So, when Facebook launched Facebook Platform to host and interface outside applications, Pincus pounced.

He founded Zynga in April 2007 as Presidio Media, with five employees, and soon renamed it after his bulldog (who also is featured in its logo). Pincus predicted the social media platform experience would benefit from social games. "I've always been a closet gamer," he said in a 2009 interview, "but I never have the time and can never get all of my friends together in one place. So the power of my friends already being there and connected, and then adding games, seemed like a big idea."[11]

Zynga's first game was Texas Hold 'Em Poker, which was also the first game to be introduced on the Facebook Platform, launched in July 2007. It was a hit. The next year, Zynga launched Mafia Wars. Its games were specifically designed to emphasize the social aspect of the host platform, engaging one's social network in gameplay. This not only increased the personalism of gameplay but also incited quicker expansion and diffusion.

By 2009, Zynga had the most active users of any Facebook developer. The same year, it acquired MyMiniLife (bringing its personnel total to *nine*), which helped them develop *FarmVille*—in a development period of only five weeks! *FarmVille* eventually reached 80 million players in 2010, and Zynga went public in 2011, raising $1 billion.

Beginning in 2012, things turned southward for Zynga. Daily active users slumped, and revenues collapsed. Reasons for this fast fall from grace aren't totally clear. Gamers abandoned Facebook and turned to mobile apps at a growing rate, and Zynga was slow in shifting with the market to the mobile platforms. By 2013, Zynga had lost almost half of its users and laid off almost a fifth of its workforce.

Amid this turmoil, Zynga's board grew frustrated with Pincus and turned to new leadership for help, handing the reins to Microsoft executive Don Mattrick. Mattrick had led Microsoft's Interactive Entertainment Business group, helping establish Microsoft as a key player in the gaming industry. Investors hoped and expected Mattrick to deliver some new hits on mobile. Not totally exiled, Pincus stayed on as chairman and chief product officer.

But Mattrick was unable to turn things around for Zynga. Active users continued to plummet, and Mattrick laid off another 15 percent of the workforce. Its best mobile hit was a retread of *FarmVille* (*FarmVille 2: Country Escape*), which was far from the hit Zynga needed. Other titles also flopped. Mattrick blamed Pincus and pushed him out of his active role with the company, though he stayed on as chairman of the board.

But Mattrick continued to make mistakes. He overhauled Zynga Poker, its most successful game, to give it a real casino feel. The active user base hated the change. Like Coca-Cola's New Coke/Coca-Cola

Classic fiasco, Zynga relented and rolled out an alternate Zynga Poker Classic with the familiar play, but the damage had been done, and both apps fell out of the top apps rankings. He spent half a billion dollars to acquire NaturalMotion, which had some hot mobile games (e.g., CSR racing, Clumsy Ninja), to try to inject some creativity. They desperately needed to generate a couple of hot new apps. But all they got were flops.

In 2015, the board had had enough, and they gave the keys back to Pincus. As chairman and controlling shareholder, Pincus had a lot to do with that decision. The next year, Pincus stepped aside again and handed the company over to Frank Gibeau, who was the head of mobile gaming at Electronic Arts. Under Gibeau, the turnaround was more successful and eventually, in 2022, Zynga was acquired by Take-Two Interactive.

LESSONS LEARNED AND MISLEARNED

In each of these cases and many more, the transition away from founder mode wasn't as smooth as investors expected. Taking the reins from the founder and handing them over to an experienced industry executive was all too often a turn for the worse.

These aren't one-off examples. The aggregate data tell a clear story—founders are better leaders. For example, a 2008 study by Lerong He revealed that "founder-managed firms are associated with higher financial performance and are more likely to survive than professional managed firms."[12]

In a 2009 study, Fahlenbrach found that the rate of return of founder-led public companies was 8.3 percent annually, with 4.4 percent excess performance above expectations.[13] Bain and Co. partners Zook and Allen detailed their research findings that founder-led firms have 31 percent more patents, more valuable patents, take smarter risks, and see consistently better performance.[14]

Furthermore, a 2020 analysis by Murugaboopathy and Dogra found that "the top 400 founder-led stocks from all sectors have registered an average share price gain of 58.4% versus a 10% return for the top 400 stocks led by others."[15] Even having (former) founders on the board has a meaningful positive effect on firm value, according to a 2022 study.[16]

There are, of course, some endogeneity and survivorship bias problems to account for, but it is on these grounds that we estimate a 50 percent productivity penalty due to administration mode in the US. In fact, our estimate is conservative. Over time, the productivity effect compounds exponentially.

The lesson to be learned here, however, is not obvious, and it's quite possible to misinterpret the data. For example, Graham recounts,

> Founders feel like they're being gaslit from both sides—by the people telling them they have to run their companies like managers, and by the people working for them when they do. Usually when everyone around you disagrees with you, your default assumption should be that you're mistaken. But this is one of the rare exceptions. VCs who haven't been founders themselves don't know how founders should run companies, and C-level execs, as a class, include some of the most skillful liars in the world.[17]

Graham is right to prefer founder mode. Founder mode employs minimal administration and instead focuses on maximizing customer value creation through entrepreneurial action. Founder mode is the empathy-informed ethical drive to identify unmet needs and address them through innovations that create new value. Companies in founder mode are customer-centric, focused deeply on their customers and their value experience. Experimentation and discovery, rather than strategies and plans, are the primary modes and methods of progress.

But it's a bit facile to believe that founder mode should just stay on all the time.

We also need good and effective management, the accumulated knowledge and guidance that brings consistency, duration, and reliability and that keeps employees engaged and intentions aligned. Well-managed companies earn investors' support and customer trust and loyalty. They avoid crises and volatility.

What we don't need is *administration.*

The problem is that these concepts are sometimes hard to disentangle, and managers often become ineffective administrators.

However, the label "founder mode" is misleading. It suggests or implies that the founder is a necessary component, and that can't always be the case, nor is it mandatory.[18] While Elon Musk is officially one of the founders of Tesla, the real founder was Martin Eberhard, along with Marc Tarpenning. One would be hard-pressed to say that the transition in leadership from Eberhard to Musk constituted a shift from founder mode to manager mode. Musk runs all of his businesses in a distinctive, entrepreneurial manner whether he's the founder or not. We call it ***venture mode.***

DIAGNOSIS

This book is a diagnosis of the problems of business administration—the running of business in what we'll call *administration mode.* It is the dominant modality in business organization today. Why do so many ventures fail to scale or sustain their growth trajectory when they transition to administration mode, turning the reins over to experienced or trained managers? What tends to happen is that managers are brought in who are experienced or trained in administration rather than in entrepreneurial leadership. This transition spells the beginning of the end for these businesses, because businesses must be persistently entrepreneurial to survive in the modern competitive landscape.

In large part, the traditional wisdom persists because very little actual training in entrepreneurial leadership exists in the world. Almost all business education is training in administration. But the benefits of administration are narrow and limited to specific cases. Some companies have demonstrated that you don't actually need it at all at any level, as we'll show later in this book. Administration is focused on efficiency and scale, and therefore, it is inherently bureaucratic, indecisive, and slow. In contrast, the modern business requires entrepreneurial leadership to innovate through the dynamism of fast-paced markets. Most businesses should *never* turn on administrator mode. But it's easy to think they should.

The core of the problem is that it's easy to think that, once a new product's value is established, once there's proof of concept, the goal of the business should be to capture that value. But this is a fundamental misunderstanding of value, one that is nurtured and propagated by economists and business school professors alike. Your product doesn't *have* value, its value isn't objective, so you can't "capture" it. Value is *subjective*: Customers *value* your product, and it is only valuable insofar as they value it. Value is a *verb*, not a noun.

It's dangerous and misleading to presume real and objective value that is there to be captured. This conflates profits or revenues with value. Revenues are, of course, the lifeblood of business, but they are secondary and derivative of value. Value creation comes first,[19] and revenues then stream in as recompense for the created value. It's much better for business leaders (and business students) to learn and understand what value *really* is and where it comes from.

With a proper understanding of value, it becomes apparent why business leaders need to be incessant entrepreneurs. While consumers like familiarity, what they really want is their best life. And while there's safety in familiar value, they'll abandon that familiar value unrepentantly for something truly better in a heartbeat.

In this book, we'll discuss what value really is and where it comes from. Then we will explain what good business leadership looks like, which includes showing just how wrong and ineffective the standard business curriculum is.

By implication, what traditional business schools teach—business administration—is mostly useless or worse. Sure, business schools (B-schools for short) teach some valuable skills, like how to read a financial statement. But our goal is to convince you that the prevailing business education paradigm has an overall negative effect on business performance. It is *worsening* business leaders' effectiveness.

One metric is revenue growth. Revenue is the result of customers' willingness to pay for the value they perceive a company is offering. So it's a decent proxy for value creation. From 2019 to 2024, the average five-year revenue growth rate for the companies in the S&P 500 was 16.5 percent. For the top five companies, it was 134.9 percent. We believe the difference points toward the superiority of venture mode over administration mode.

We hope to convince you of our thesis with theoretical and logical arguments, backed up by real-life examples. Once the logical flaws of the current paradigm are made manifest, it becomes clear how and why standard business practices are suboptimal.

The obvious implication is for a paradigm shift in business thinking and therefore in business education. This is precisely what we hope to achieve, so we'll invite your consideration of a completely new form of business education for a post-administration era. It will be founded on the well-established principles of entrepreneurial economics that have long been left outside of business school curricula. Even the entrepreneurship curricula in B-schools are teaching an administrative view of entrepreneurship.

OUR GOALS

Our goals in this book are to:

1. Describe venture mode as an alternative to administration for running a business;
2. Show you *why* venture mode should always stay on;
3. Explain *how* to keep venture mode on;
4. Point the finger at business school curricula and scholarship as the primary culprits for the commonality and persistence of administration mode; and
5. Propose a solution that we hope will inspire you to join us in a project toward a new business education paradigm.

The new business education paradigm will embed a true entrepreneurial mindset within a new generation of value creators, allowing them to lead businesses persistently in venture mode. Venture mode, not administration, is the key to unleashing a new high-productivity future.

CHAPTER 2

ADMINISTRATION MODE

What does business as usual mean to you? As an idiom, it just means maintaining the status quo by keeping to the same old routine. But business as usual is administration.

Merely maintaining the status quo can be fatal for businesses if they don't adapt to the marketplace changes going on around them. Yet businesses have been primarily led by administrators since time immemorial. Effectively, that is what kingship and lordship are—administration. Over centuries, administration has become the norm for managing big, bureaucratic organizations from governments to companies. Aspiring business leaders train to become administrators.

No doubt, administration has its place. The world needs *some* administrators. Or, perhaps we should say, we need some people to do administrative tasks—to oversee a job and make sure it gets done, done right, and done well. But we don't need administrators in business leadership roles.

Why not? To answer this question, we need to dig into the purpose of a business executive—what makes them good or great in that role?

Instinctively, we generally think it has to be about *leadership*, that a business executive must lead and inspire to accomplish great things. That's not wrong *per se*, but leading others isn't the fundamental purpose of a business executive.

The fundamental purpose of a business executive is *entrepreneurship*. In economics, "entrepreneurship" or the "entrepreneurial function" is the task of determining *what to do* with one's resources, to seek out the best possible uses for them. That's the job of the executive, the strategic manager. It's their job to decide *what to do*. And it's no easy task.

The *best* possible use of resources is actually a fiction—there is no *best*, there's only *better*. The *best* possible use hasn't been discovered yet and won't ever be. There will always be something even better to discover. But that's the job of the strategic executive, the entrepreneurial leader—to find even *better* ways to use the company's resources, to create even more value for their customers and, consequently, themselves.

Being a true entrepreneurial leader requires the spirit of entrepreneurship and the creative embrace of uncertainty. The best entrepreneurial leaders imbue this same entrepreneurial spirit in every individual, team, group, division, function, process, method, and metric within their care and impart a vision of possibility for the world to aspire to.

Instead, what too many executives actually do is administration. You never want an administrator at the head because administration is bureaucracy and stagnation, which spells doom to any business in the long run.

WHAT IS ADMINISTRATION MODE?

As we showed in chapter one, this point was effectively made first by Brian Chesky, cofounder and former CEO of Airbnb, at a Y

Combinator retreat in 2024. The talk came on the heels of a massive restructuring at Airbnb a year earlier. The company terminated a large swath of middle management, and Chesky became more centrally involved, assuming the role of chief product officer.

The origins of his talk on founder mode resulted from Airbnb's growing pains with figuring out its organizational structure. It's a familiar story of the challenges of organizational design. The "simple structure" that small businesses often have works great. In business school jargon, these small organizations thrive on an "organic" structure that facilitates innovation and agility. Such a structure also engenders a strong culture of accountability because the company is small and tight-knit—everyone works closely with each other, and the founder is just a step away.

But as a company grows larger and more complex, the start-up team often feels forced to adopt a more complicated organizational structure—typically a functional structure (normally with a divisional segmentation) or perhaps a matrix structure if it's a global organization (with geographic managers who deal with international differences and other challenges).

Such were the growing pains Airbnb was experiencing, as Chesky recounted in a 2024 interview:

> From 2009 to 2019, I ran Airbnb the way most tech companies run their companies. I didn't know how to run it, so I hired people from Google, Amazon, Microsoft, and other companies, and they brought their processes with them. We kind of reverted towards the way everyone runs their company.

He recounted the frustrations of their Creative Group, a team tasked with creating graphics for the rest of the business. As Airbnb expanded and staffed a bunch of subteams, the asks on the Creative Group started to pile up. Chesky recalled, "If you needed anything done, let's say you . . . needed a button designed, or a graphic for a button design, it would be like a three-month waiting list because they were inundated."

As the company grew, Airbnb started to subdivide into a functional structure.

> The problem with that, though, is that once you subdivide the company, the company starts rowing in different directions. Now, you have even more bureaucracy because the groups don't want to work together. They're incentivized to work on different things, and they might not be totally compatible anymore. Ten teams can have ten different tech stacks, and they don't actually fit together. A local decision that might make sense for your team might not make sense for the company.

Challenges with aligning incentives lead to organizational politicking. Accountability becomes particularly difficult—a heavy hand to build accountability tends to result in a toxic culture. You need oversight, but employees don't like having a micromanager looking over their shoulders. At the same time, if you don't crack down on poor performance, that too can become toxic.

Chesky explained,

> If I could summarize founder mode in a couple sentences, it's about being in the details. It's that great leadership is presence, not absence. It's about a leader being in the details. And if you as a leader aren't in the details, guess what? Your leaders aren't in the details, and their leaders

> aren't in the details. And one day you're going to wake up, and you have fifty-year-olds managing forty-year-olds, managing thirty-year-olds, managing people two years out of college doing all the work with no oversight, and you have these four unnecessary layers. You have no experts in the company.[1]

Here he gets at the core of founder mode and, conversely, administration mode. Let's unpack the problems Chesky was exposing.

MANAGER MODE

What we're calling *administration mode* was originally coined as *manager mode* by Paul Graham.[2] When new ventures reach proof of concept and it's time to hit the gas, traditional wisdom says that they need experienced managers to take the reins. Graham states,

> In effect there are two different ways to run a company: founder mode and manager mode. Till now most people even in Silicon Valley have implicitly assumed that scaling a startup meant switching to manager mode.[3]

Manager mode is the phase that businesses enter in order to streamline, cut costs, and scale. Flipping to manager mode after the proof-of-concept stage is conventional wisdom because competitiveness intensifies in this phase. Once people realize that there's market value in a new product, a slew of imitators jump into the industry as quickly as they can to try to cash in on the wave.

To survive and stay ahead, ventures need to turn the heat up, scale quickly, drive down costs (and maybe prices), and build the brand. The prevailing thought is that founders aren't the right leaders for this transitional stage. They don't have enough experience or administrative know-how. It's better to turn the reins over to an experienced industry manager who can get the company to scale quickly.

Manager mode comprises endless how-to books, articles, podcasts, and other forms of disseminated scholarship on leadership, organization, and efficiency. Successful business leaders throughout the decades have written their stories of how they did it, what worked, what didn't, and what they learned along the way. At the same time, management scholars in universities have pursued the same how-to questions through a scientific process. They've collected and analyzed data from businesses across the globe to identify the causal factors, mechanisms, and processes that enabled some firms to achieve success where others failed. Thousands of academic publications, along with the anecdotal stories from those who succeed, paint a nice picture of effective business administration.

The problem with this, for Chesky, is that if you turn your company over to professional managers, you no longer have an expert who knows the intricacies of the product. Chesky took particular inspiration from Steve Jobs on this. In a 1985 interview, Jobs observed,

> You know who the best managers are? They're the great individual contributors who never ever want to be a manager, but decide they have to be a manager because no one else is going to be able to do as good a job as that.[4]

Chesky took this to heart. The leaders of the organization need to be experts, people who know what they're doing and what they're talking about, people who inspire. In his words,

> Your leaders shouldn't just be "managers" (and I put managers in quotes), they should also be in the details. If we

> were a military, like a battalion, the cavalry general should know how to ride a horse. It's crazy that they don't. And leaders shouldn't be fungible. So it's really about being in the details.[5]

Graham echoes this:

> The way managers are taught to run companies seems to be like modular design in the sense that you treat subtrees of the org chart as black boxes. You tell your direct reports what to do, and it's up to them to figure out how. But you don't get involved in the details of what they do. That would be micromanaging them, which is bad. . . . The CEO should engage with the company only via his or her direct reports.[6]

The problem of micromanagement is a tricky one. But being in the details doesn't have to mean micromanagement. Jobs explains,

> The greatest people are self-managing—they don't need to be managed. Once they know what to do, they'll figure it out. What they need is a common vision and that's what leadership is. What leadership is is having a vision, being able to articulate that so the people around you can understand it, and getting a consensus on a common vision.[7]

But what tends to happen is that the organization turns to professional administrators instead of product experts for various reasons. Often, this new leadership is experienced—not necessarily in the specific product or even industry, but they bring a wealth of knowledge and experience about running and scaling a large business. This is manager mode. As a result, leadership oversees strategy and efficiency, but they don't know the details of the products they make or the processes involved.

It's the job of the administrator—the professional manager—to make sure tasks are completed efficiently and effectively with every detail adhering to the predetermined plan and process. But effective management often means giving employees some leeway to accomplish their tasks as they see fit and make creative deviations when they identify a benefit in doing so. Administrators often do not have enough knowledge or experience to know specifically how something should be done or how it could be done better, so it is often preferable to let those who know more make the call. But this would require the administrator to relinquish some control, which seems risky.

Even a founder can shift to manager mode. Chesky explains, "What a lot of founders do is they let go of the product, and they abdicate responsibility."[8]

There is intuitive appeal and history to support the conventional wisdom. Many businesses *did* succeed by switching to manager mode. But, of course, as Chesky, Graham, and others have astutely observed, this conventional wisdom doesn't seem to be working out all that well today. Did something change? Was the conventional wisdom just an artifact, a result of survivorship bias? Did it ever really work?

ADMINISTRATION MODE

Why do we use the term *administration mode* instead of Paul Graham's "manager mode"? Terminology is important. *Management* is broadly used to signify business leadership. Founders or experienced industry heads are all called *managers*.

The problematic approach that Chesky identified is more accurately termed *administration*. It is focused on operational effectiveness, on improving processes. *Administration* clearly connotes what Chesky meant in his remarks. We also prefer the term because it helps us point the finger at one of its key sources: the business school. Business schools bestow degrees in business *administration*, and it's the right word for what they teach. Business schools have been factories of administrators for almost a century, though we'll dig into the history and specifics of their curriculum in the next chapter.

HOW HAS ADMINISTRATION MODE WORKED OUT?

The mainstream supposition that businesses should be administered via "scientific" methods has proven faulty time and again. But the idea generally refuses to die. It's ingrained in the *logos* and perhaps even the *ethos* of global business. In part, this is because administration mode often works *for a time*. Short-term profitability *can* be improved by good administration. But in the long run, it always fails because administration is an impediment to entrepreneurship.

This radical claim is borne out by anecdote after anecdote. Eventually, so many anecdotes constitute informative data, but let's consider a few more closely.

In Paul Graham's blog post about Chesky, he shares,

> Hire good people and give them room to do their jobs. Sounds great when it's described that way, doesn't it? Except in practice, judging from the report of founder after founder, what this often turns out to mean is: hire professional fakers and let them drive the company into the ground.

Graham has it a bit wrong here. They're not "fakers." They're administrators. They can run a tight ship. But you don't need someone who runs a tight ship when the winds change or the waters get choppy. You need someone who can figure out where to steer the ship. If you don't have that visionary leader, the inevitable winds of change will push you off course to your inevitable doom.

Apple's Bout with Administration Mode

We already shared Airbnb's run-in with administration mode. Decades earlier, Apple had a bout with administration mode also, even before Steve Jobs was pushed out. Jobs saw the problem—in fact, it likely had to do with his ousting, as Jobs's strategic vision for the company disagreed with the conventional wisdom that permeated the top brass.

Jobs recounts,

> We went through that stage in Apple when we went out and we thought, "Oh, we're going to be a big company. Let's hire professional management." We went out and hired a bunch of professional management. It didn't work at all. Most of them were bozos. They knew how to manage, but they didn't know how to do anything.

At the time, Jobs was running the Macintosh project at Apple. But his differences in strategic vision (and his apparent combativeness) led to his dismissal. His departure signaled Apple's full entrance into administration mode, focused on streamlining and cutting costs. But, rather ironically, the Macintosh that Jobs and team developed would be the only product keeping Apple afloat during this phase. Its other projects all floundered.

Jobs's triumphal return, which spelled the end of Apple's administrative phase, also famously sparked the biggest turnaround in modern business history. In fact, it was Jobs's turnaround, his rejection of administration mode in favor of venture mode, that inspired Chesky at Airbnb to do the same.

Xerox and the Palo Alto Research Center

Another interesting example is Xerox, the copier company. In 1969, Xerox's chairman, C. Peter McColough, tasked the chief scientist, Jack Goldman, to solve the "architecture of information" problem created by the "knowledge explosion" of the time.[9] Xerox had just bought Scientific Data Systems, which manufactured computer mainframes. Goldman turned to physicist and friend George Pake, and, together, they founded the Palo Alto Research Center (or PARC) on the opposite coast from Xerox headquarters in Palo Alto, California, in 1970.

Whether the distance from corporate headquarters was intentional or not, its three thousand-mile separation from corporate executives enabled PARC researchers to pursue their visions of the future mostly unfettered by corporate bureaucracy. Pake, who headed the group, recruited Bob Taylor from the University of Utah, who had previously run ARPA for the military,[10] and together they recruited a team of all-star scientists. It's generally acknowledged that about half of the world's top one hundred computer scientists at the time worked at PARC.

Pake, Taylor, and their team set out to create the office of the future for Xerox. The culture was one of systems thinking and user focus. One team member, Alan Kay, recalled, "One of the blood oaths that was taken by the original founders was that we would never do a system that wasn't engineered for 100 users."[11]

By late 1972, they began working on the Alto computer, arguably the first personal computer prototype, which they completed in a mere five months. Eventually, the team would also develop the Smalltalk system—a graphical user interface that featured overlapping "windows." The concept of windows and the trackball mouse were not created by PARC researchers, but they were the first to develop them into a functional technology for broad usership.

They also built modern Ethernet technology and the first laser printer. They made huge advancements in computer language and programming, including object-oriented programming. The PARC team built the modern computer world.

But, of course, we look at the world of computers today, and Xerox's name is nowhere to be seen. In 1976, PARC leadership went to the Xerox executives and pitched the development of a mass-market version of the Alto called the Alto III. Xerox turned it down.

Kay recalled, "Xerox management had been told early on that Altos at PARC were like Kleenex; they would be used up in three years and we would need a new set of things 10 times faster."[12]

The next year, the PARC researchers were invited to a big corporate event where they were asked to demonstrate the technologies they had developed. By most accounts, the presentation went over well. But executives still did nothing with the technology. The organization was too disorganized, too bureaucratic to bring the technology to market.

PARC researcher Larry Tesler said, "The last year before I left PARC I spent flying around the country talking to Xerox executives, carrying Notetaker with me. It was the first portable computer run in an airport. Xerox executives made all sorts of promises: we'll buy 20,000, just talk to this executive in Virginia, then talk to this executive in Connecticut. The company was so spread out, they never got the meeting together. After a year I was ready to give up."[13]

Meanwhile, Xerox's corporate offices in New York generally saw PARC as a bit of a madcap bunch. Richard Shoup recalled, "PARC was a very strange place to the rest of the company. It was not only California, but it was nerds. It was thought of as weird computer people who had beards, who didn't bathe or wear shoes, who spent long hours deep into the night staring at their terminals, who had no relationships with any other human beings, and who basically were antisocial eggheads. Frankly, some of us fed that impression, as if we were above the rest of the company."[14]

PARC researchers grew frustrated, and many of them left to join other companies or start their own. Then, in 1979, Steve Jobs was given a privileged demonstration of the Smalltalk system. PARC researcher Adele Goldberg, who was asked to deliver the demonstration, was furious with Xerox management, arguing that they were about to "give away the kitchen sink."[15] She was right. Jobs knew instantly that the graphical user interface was how all computers would work someday and immediately set to work on the Macintosh design.

Kodak's Bureaucracy

Eastman Kodak, founded in 1880, developed the first snapshot camera in 1888. Using the razor blade business model developed by King Gillette, Kodak sold its cameras at a steep discount, making them affordable for the masses, while most of their revenues came from repeat film purchases.[16] In 1962, it reached $1 billion in sales. By 1996, Eastman Kodak was the fourth most valuable brand in the US. Yet in 2012, it filed for bankruptcy.

A common myth is that Kodak failed because it missed the digital photography revolution. That's not true. In fact, Kodak invented the first megapixel sensor in 1986, and it introduced over fifty products related to digital images. Another telling of the story concludes that Kodak sat on the tech, scared to cannibalize its own film sales. That version of the story is only partially true. The real story of Kodak's demise is their turn to administration mode.

Kodak went through seven restructurings in a decade, from 1983 to 1993, under Colby Chandler and then Kay Whitmore.[17] In 1988, the company diversified into pharmaceuticals, acquiring Sterling Drug for $5.1 billion. That same year, it also bought IBM's photocopier business.

When Whitmore took over in 1990, he wanted to refocus the organization, spinning off its chemical business. In 1993, Whitmore stepped down and handed the reins to George Fisher, a professional manager famous for turning around Motorola—the first time in Kodak's long history to hire an outsider as CEO. The board was particularly intrigued by Fisher's experience in technology, hoping he could keep Kodak on track with the changing technological landscape.

But Fisher was a professional administrator. His first move was to refocus Kodak on photography. By 1996, Kodak had cut $50 million in production costs and significantly reduced cycle times. Fisher was a genius at streamlining—right at the moment that the industry was shifting hard toward digital technology. Fisher was convinced that film was not dying, seeing China in particular as a big emerging market for film—he even invested heavily in a joint venture with the CCP.[18] But film photography collapsed much quicker than Fisher anticipated, and in 2000, Fisher was pushed aside for Daniel Carp.

But by this time, Kodak was already behind the curve and had to play catch-up in an organization that had grown bureaucratic. Still, it had a lot of resources, so the company tried to make up ground by buying its way forward. For example, it acquired online picture service Ofoto in 2002 and picture archiving and communication systems developer Algotech in 2003. In 2004, it discontinued film cameras in North America and Europe, focusing fully on digital cameras.

Carp also tried to recreate corporate culture, recruiting experienced digital technologists to accelerate technology development. To do this, he increased the pressure on his team. Business analyst Ulysses Yannas reported, "In the past, when a guy was given a task and he wouldn't perform, they'd move him someplace else. Carp essentially changed that by telling people, 'You have a year to do the job. You don't do it, you're out the door.'"[19] But it wasn't happening fast enough.

In 2005, Carp stepped down and was replaced by Antonio Perez, who doubled down on the move to digital. Perez explained, "Our plan is to finish this year with slightly higher revenue from digital than from analog, but still two-thirds of profit will come from the analog business. Those numbers will be changing significantly. . . . That's why we call the next two years as the critical years."[20]

But their digital technologies never caught up with the competition. Perez tried diversifying, investing heavily in printers and workplace software. But Kodak was burning through cash quickly. They sold off assets and cut the workforce, but nothing was paying off. Eventually, Perez took to lawsuits, which also didn't pay off.[21]

Paul Porter, Kodak's director of design and usability, commented,

> We were way ahead of the curve in digital even though we were pretty much a film and chemical company. We did a lot of research in digital because we knew at some point in time the world would change. We invented the digital camera. So, being the first ones there we continuously worked in the labs so to make sure when that change was made we were prepared for it. So we have the expertise in the research labs to generate these innovations that make our experience either, more gratifying, more intuitive or better connected than what other people do.[22]

Yet, despite being technologically ahead of the game for years, Kodak couldn't adapt quickly enough because it was in administration mode.

General Motors

General Motors (GM) was the epitome of administration. It was a bureaucracy that had bloated incrementally over a century, culminating finally in its bankruptcy amid the financial crisis in 2009. It's a marvel that it had survived so long, all things considered.

In the wake of the bankruptcy, Steven Rattner was tasked by the Obama administration to assess the situation. He reported, "Everyone knew Detroit's reputation for insular, slow-moving cultures. Even by that low standard, I was shocked by the stunningly poor management that we found."[23]

In 1988, GM senior executive Elmer Johnson wrote an internal memo: "We have not achieved the success that we must because of severe limitations on our organization's ability to execute in a timely manner. . . . We have vastly underestimated how [deeply] ingrained are the organizational and cultural rigidities that hamper our ability to execute."

This administrative culture, he noted, arose out of assumptions, embraced after World War II, that "we live in a very stable, reasonably predictable world," and that "GM's overwhelming competitive advantage lies to a large degree in its ability to achieve monumental economies of scale."[24] Like most companies who shift into administration mode, these assumptions hold true for a time. Until they don't.

GM's administrative culture persisted, despite Johnson's warning. By the mid-2000s, GM's employees were evaluated multiple times each year for their compliance to a job description that was "spelled out in exhaustive detail" using a "performance measurement process" that "could fill a three-ring binder."[25]

Rattner's report continued, "The cultural deficiencies were equally stunning. At GM's Renaissance Center headquarters, the top brass were sequestered on the uppermost floor, behind locked and guarded glass doors. Executives housed on that floor had elevator cards that allowed them to descend to their private garage without stopping at any of the intervening floors (no mixing with the drones)."[26]

The bankruptcy enabled GM to make some desperately needed changes. But administration was still the name of the game in the auto industry. That is, until Tesla came around. Today, auto industry incumbents are fighting for survival, which has necessitated a shift out of administration mode.

MODERN BUSINESS IS TOO DYNAMIC FOR ADMINISTRATION MODE

What we've concluded from our analysis is that administration mode doesn't work for most businesses. And it's apparent from the buzz that followed Brian Chesky's comments that a lot of other business leaders and investors see it too. But what's also clear is that it's not obvious *why* administration mode doesn't work. Intuitively, administration mode makes a lot of sense. But while some have tried to explain why, their explanations have been (admittedly) guesses.

Our explanation is unique and powerful because we have a very different view of the economy, of business, and of entrepreneurship from most. Our analytical tool is subjectivism, the philosophy of science that understands human/social sciences (like economics) as altogether different animals from the natural sciences. This view has led us to alternative theories of economics (such as the so-called "Austrian school of economics"), entrepreneurship, and management that we think offer a much better understanding of the business problem that Chesky and Graham illuminated.

From our subjectivist vantage, the reason businesses shouldn't switch to administration mode is because it turns off venture mode—the mode in which founders like Chesky and investors like Graham conceived of and launched their innovative, value-creating businesses. Administration mode stifles creativity and innovation in favor of uniformity, predictability, and bureaucracy. And *all* businesses need venture mode permanently switched on to survive long term.

Our point of view is different from most others, but we are also persuaded that it's *right*. We don't have answers to everything, but seeing through this lens of subjectivist economics results in a focus and understanding that can't be gleaned from within the orthodoxy. But once you see it, you can't unsee it.

CHAPTER 3

THE MBA

Let's turn now to the chief villain of our argument—the business school. We admit that it's controversial to claim that the business school—and its fabrication of over two hundred thousand MBAs every year[1]—is the main culprit of administration mode. Especially given that one of us teaches in a business school!

Certainly, we can't lay *all* the blame at the feet of the MBA curriculum. But business school studies also generate the academic work of the so-called business discipline and corresponding pop-press books and articles by academics who study the "scientific" (i.e., evidence-based) way to do business. And we would also include those success story write-ups by good and well-meaning business leaders who share their secrets with the masses. They often seem to be chasing the incentive of renown that comes from claiming the origination of "best practices."

The problem with this modern culture of business thinking and business education is that all these learning channels generate a sense of right and wrong, of good and bad, of better and worse in business practice. "This is the *right* way to do business." "This way *works*, where other ways often fail." And the more evidence is accumulated, the more this sentiment embroils the business culture. Consequently, business is seen as a machine to be optimized and fine-tuned, which is done following a checklist of best practices—and the person for this job is a capable *administrator.*

Historically, an MBA degree from a top business school has virtually guaranteed the holder a high-paying career, starting at an advanced and privileged position on the corporate ladder. The business school is perceived by hiring corporations as providing an invaluable service of finding, vetting, and training the best and brightest of minds interested in business leadership.

These students are indeed bright and talented, capable of greatness. But they're steeped in business *administration*. Supposedly, they come out of school armed with the analytical tools and training of the cutting edge of management science. In actuality, most of what they learn is far from cutting edge, but it's still widely accepted.

MBA graduates permeate the corporate landscape. It's understandable—that's what they trained for after all. So one might argue that perhaps MBAs make the best leaders and that's why they rise to the top. There may be some truth to this idea, although we're skeptical. Nevertheless, MBAs and middle managers get promoted for their skills in administration. That's what middle managers do. And that's why MBAs are brought in—they are trained in administration. When these able administrators finally make their way to the top, they have demonstrated their aptitude for administration. But businesses don't need an administrator as their strategic leader—they need an entrepreneur.

How and why did administration become the focus of the business school and thus become so entrenched in modern business culture? Let's run through the history and some recent trends regarding the MBA. When we do, we'll see diminishing value. The MBA isn't worth what it once was—savvy businesses are figuring out the problems with administrative leadership and are now looking for new approaches.

Why Is Administration Mode So Common?

A looming question is, How did administration mode become so popular if it doesn't work? Why is it standard operating procedure to get to administration mode as soon as possible in order to scale? And then to maintain administration mode for a business of any significant size? Is it possible that administration mode has its place?

Perhaps administration has a place *within* an organization (though Chesky disputes even this). But it definitely doesn't belong at the top. So why do business schools teach it in the way they do?

Why Do Business Schools Teach Administration?

Business schools (or B-schools) are part of an academic community that is expected to generate new scientific knowledge. Essentially, the B-school is expected to teach the cutting edge of management science—what business scholars have learned from thousands of studies of business practices and performance.

The issue here is that a *scientific* approach to business management is inherently administrative. It develops "best practices" from aggregated examples according to their past performance. These best practices are then formalized into the curriculum and are taught to B-school students. In other words, a scientific approach to business inevitably becomes a checklist approach, the best way to run a tight business. That is, it produces an administration curriculum.

Why Are B-Schools to Blame for Administration Mode?

Academia is held up as the pinnacle of human knowledge. Being trained at a university suggests that one is trained up to the edge of contemporary knowledge. Medical doctors are (supposedly) trained in the latest and greatest of medical science. Engineers are trained in the latest science and methods of technological development. Business students are trained in the latest and greatest science of administration.

Companies continue to turn to B-schools for recruiting and then train those graduates up to what they need them to actually do. Why? Why not skip the costly and yet ineffective education and just move right to on-the-job training? Well, there are a few, like Peter Thiel, who have proposed that businesses do just that. However, for the most part, hiring corporations believe that the B-school still provides a useful function: intelligence screening.

It's generally frowned upon, even illegal in many places, to give an intelligence screening exam in the hiring process. Yet most companies still want to hire the most talented and capable they can get. They want the most intelligent. They want hard workers. They want people who can get a task done on time and done well. And, as it turns out, universities provide this sort of screening for them.

Economist Bryan Caplan, in his book *The Case Against Education*, argues that the real value of a university diploma is in the signal that it sends to employers. Studies suggest that most students graduate having actually learned (retained) almost nothing. So what are they spending four-plus years and tens of thousands of dollars for?

Well, a great many employers require a diploma for job positions. Why? Because to earn a diploma you first need to score well on the SAT (or other entrance exam) and pass a bunch of classes (which requires deference to a professor, some intelligence, and sufficient diligence to stay committed to the completion of the course).

In other words, to receive a diploma, you need to show that you can act like a good employee. So employers use this as a predictive signal of likely employee quality. The more competitive schools offer stronger signals since you must be really smart and hardworking to be admitted into those schools in the first place, much less finish.

But while the B-school diploma remains valuable, a side effect is the training these graduates get in administration and administrative thinking. While students don't retain much, the *mindset* instilled and nurtured by B-schools is lasting. And it's the wrong mindset for business.

Administration is traditionally viewed as quite valuable in middle management—MBAs often make great middle managers. But middle management is increasingly identified as a problem area for business. In an email to Tesla employees, Elon Musk decried middle managers' tendency to slow progress:

> There are two schools of thought about how information should flow. By far the most common way is chain of command, which means that you always flow communication through your manager. The problem with this approach is that, while it enhances the power of the manager, it fails to serve the company. To solve a problem quickly, two people in different depts should simply talk and make the right thing happen. Instead, people are forced to talk to their manager, who talks to their manager, who talks to the manager in the other dept, who talks to someone on his team. Then the info has to flow back the other way again. This is incredibly dumb.[2]

Worse, when great administrators demonstrate they can run a tight ship, they get promoted out of middle management and into top management. And that's how firms get themselves into administration mode.

We're not saying that internal promotion is always a terrible idea. In fact, some of the greatest entrepreneurs and innovators of our time earned an MBA, and some of them were even middle managers first. But more often than not, business leaders are promoted for their administrative prowess, and not for their entrepreneurial vision.

HOW DID WE GET HERE?

So how did B-schools become the wellspring of administration? Well, business schools started with the wrong philosophy. It may be unconventional to link business and philosophy, but the connection is fundamental. And there's an interesting philosophical backstory to the entrenchment of administration in B-schools.

The Rise of Positivism

During the Enlightenment, Europe emerged as the central hub of academia. It was where all the important academic conversations and debates were happening. France in particular emerged as a premier academic hub, with two Parisian universities of particular note and renown. These two universities, separated by about twenty-five kilometers (15.5 miles), are both a reflection and a microcosm of the debates over the philosophy of science that would unfold over the next two centuries.

First was the Collège de France, which focused on the human sciences: biology, psychology, and "ideology," the science of ideas, including what we today call sociology and economics. These "ideologues" departed sharply from the positivists' reverence for the scientific method and its capacity to answer all questions. They instead saw fundamental differences and difficulties in the human sciences—conscious and thinking people are much harder to understand and predict than unthinking rocks and planets.

The ideologues at the Collège de France were politically liberal and highly critical of Napoleon Bonaparte in his empire-building efforts. This, of course, didn't sit very well with the emperor. Napoleon not only widely criticized the scholars—his feud with them is how the modern term *ideologue* became a term of derision—but also banned the publication and teaching of their scholarship in France. The extensive work of the ideologues was very nearly cast into the dustbin of history, and Napoleon's efforts severely hampered and weakened the global influence of the scholars.

Despite this, their work didn't go totally unnoticed. Thomas Jefferson, who was for years the US ambassador to France, was an acolyte of the ideologues and even published some of their works in the US. But for the most part, their work was effectively squelched.

This was a setback for the philosophy of science. The core of ideology was a recognition that social science is fundamentally distinct from the natural sciences. It was the study of *human ideation*, of how we creatively think and act.

Antoine Destutt de Tracy delineated ideology as pertaining to four key human faculties: perception, memory, judgment, and volition. These constituted the foundations of what we today would call a *subjectivist* philosophy of social science. But it was more than a century later that his work was taken up by Austrian philosophers Wilhelm Dilthey[3] and Franz Brentano.[4]

Dilthey stressed the role of interpretation and understanding as central to the social scientists' grasp of human action. That is, the positivists were wrong to claim that scientists can ascertain the causes of human action from observation. On the contrary, they must ascertain (and understand) the *reasons* behind the action. These reasons are personal and subjective and so are quite difficult to understand. They must be interpreted. The principles of interpretation (*Verstehen*) must be applied to all of the social sciences and to understanding human action generally.

Brentano focused on intentionality—the action of the mind. Intentionality plays a central role in perception. We perceive reality *indirectly* through the filter of our interpretive intentionality. This is why different people see the same things, even objective facts, differently.

But intentionality is also the source of action. It is the decider, the chooser of values and preferences.

These Austrian philosophers are well regarded today, but they gained little traction in their time. The cultural climate of the nineteenth century was very much against them, as was the French emperor.

The second key university in our history was the École Polytechnique, a technical school, focused on the hard (natural) sciences. The school employed mathematicians, physicists, and chemists famed throughout the world. The École Polytechnique's work was vital to Napoleon's war efforts, which won them significant funding and accolades. This proved to have a lasting effect on the development of science.

Henri de Saint-Simon was a fervent acolyte of the school. He had a devout religious faith in scientific progressivism. The language we use here is not metaphorical—he was literally religiously devoted to science. He espoused a religion of science, with Sir Isaac Newton as its patron saint. In an 1803 tract—his first publication—he suggested a "Council of Newton," composed of twenty-one renowned scientists and artists elected to be God's representatives on earth, who would devise a new world order through scientific technocracy.

This religious fervor would become his philosophy of science: *positivism*. The essence of this worldview is that all mysteries of the universe can be fully unraveled through scientific inquiry. There is nothing outside of its study, and society will progressively advance with the development of science and its technologies.[5]

After Saint-Simon's death, the torch of positivism was carried by his group of young disciples. With the Saint-Simonians' proselytizing, positivism spread quickly across Europe, expedited by the exciting and increasingly rapid advances within the natural sciences. In particular, the movement took Germany by storm, influencing German writers and scholars, including Karl Marx. Expectations abounded that scientific governance would soon render the world a paradise for all.[6]

Meanwhile, in the US, the culture of innovation also proved a fertile breeding ground for a growing scientific reverence. The physicists and mathematicians in Europe were widely translated, read, and admired in the US. Consequently, the European positivist proclivities spilled over into the US and caught on like wildfire. By the twentieth century, American universities were even more positivist than the European schools.

The sentiment of the time was an immense optimism that science would soon solve all the world's problems and that brilliant technocrats would engineer a new and better world.

The Onset of Management Science

At the turn of the twentieth century, this was the academic climate in which *management science* emerged within academia. The discipline kickstarted with Frederick Taylor's 1914 book, *The Principles of Scientific Management*, where Taylor laid out a clearly positivist view of business administration. Business managers, Taylor argued, should be able to engineer maximum efficiency through carefully derived scientific principles. The book was a hit, and business management emerged as its own discipline.

A further reinforcement for positivism in the US was the influx of European academics after the two world wars. American universities welcomed the influx of the world's top minds. Taylor's scientific management ballooned in popularity and soon spawned a new generation of management scholars. Among these, Herbert Simon was particularly influential. Simon found positivism at the University of Chicago and recalled in his memoir, "More or less weekly, those friends who were especially interested in philosophy of science gathered in our apartment. . . . Logical positivism was the dominant, perhaps exclusive, religion in this group, and we took turns talking about our special interests or projects."[7]

This brings us to a pivotal moment in the story. It was Simon's book *Administrative Behavior*, first published in 1945, that would become the seminal textbook for the modern business school curriculum. Simon's work, an outgrowth of Taylor's, was fundamentally a scientific, i.e., administrative approach to business management. The focus on administration was quite overt, as the title of the book suggests. He taught that management scholars can develop proven tools and techniques to engineer better performance and efficiency.

Simon's influence remains strong and pervasive throughout the business schools of the world. *Administrative Behavior* is no longer the textbook curriculum for today's business courses, but it set the stage for the administration curriculum we still see today. Students still learn administration—tools and techniques to administrate effectively. This curriculum is a scientific program, built on the large scientific literature around the factors, methods, and processes that engender superior business performance so that we can teach those principles to students and send them out to replicate them.

ISN'T THERE ENTREPRENEURSHIP IN THE B-SCHOOL TOO?

Entrepreneurship has grown rapidly within B-schools. It's hot. It's sexy. Communities want it. Donors want it. And so university administrators want it. Most schools offer entrepreneurship courses, many offer entrepreneurship as a minor, and some even offer it as a major.

But only very few business schools emphasize and try to actually instill an *entrepreneurial* mindset. And even those few who try, teach it largely from a positivist position. That is, they teach the science of entrepreneurship, attempting to scientifically engineer better entrepreneurial processes and outcomes, à la Taylor and Simon.

However, entrepreneurship theory teaches that such efforts are foolhardy. Here's where the choice of philosophy is fundamentally important. Entrepreneurship theory is subjectivist—a direct and complete rejection of positivism.

This isn't to say that there's no overlap between science and entrepreneurship, that science is worthless to business and that businesses should avoid scientific study or data analysis. To the contrary, some recent evidence suggests that scientific approaches to business can be effective, if done well,[8] and some have made compelling arguments that this even extends to entrepreneurship.[9]

But subjectivist philosophy says that there are severe limits to what such efforts can in fact tell us. People are not statistics, and you can't understand your customer with big data. You can get some general insights, but your customers are *intentional* and *learning* beings. What they did in the past is often not a great predictor of what they'll do in the future. We like familiar value, but we also constantly search for *better value.*

In the end, entrepreneurs succeed insofar as their *customers* decide they should. Customers decide for themselves based on the value they expect from their purchase. There is no scientific method to perfect this—business success is an uncertain venture that's much more about empathy, creative ingenuity, passion, hustle, and even some luck, rather than the scientific method. It emerges from venture mode.

But B-schools typically teach students the opposite—that you should collect a lot of data, do a lot of testing and analyses, and follow the evidence. Data and analyses are useful but far more limited than scholars believe. Again, the data we're talking about are people's values and beliefs, which are actually quite fickle.

THE EVIDENCE ON MBAS

It's true that getting an MBA moves you up on that corporate ladder. But does it actually prepare you to lead a business effectively? Let's be "scientific" for a moment and utilize some data.

Let's go back to 1987. In that year, *Business Week* published a top-1,000 ranking of US businesses based on market capitalization. Of the 1,000 CEOs represented, 201 held an MBA. For comparison, 105 never finished college, including 41 who never attended.

Rose and Wong describe this as evidence that the MBA is "the dominant leadership degree" as it was the most common.[10] But given that MBAs are designed to teach business leadership, this one-in-five ratio is actually remarkably lower than one might expect. If only a fifth of tech's lead software engineers had a degree in computer science, we might rightfully wonder why computer science programs weren't producing the top software engineers and why untrained programmers were outperforming the trained ones.

Dan Rasmussen and Haonan Li put it this way:

> Surely it is better to invest in the star CEO who has a record of stunning returns than a schmuck who has underperformed the S&P. Better still if the star was forged in the crucible of Harvard Business School. There is a big market for books about these genius CEOs and how they achieved their success—and what lessons corporate executives and investors should take away from the histories of "great men.[11]

The siren songs of credentialism and tales of corporate "great men" are seductive. It is the pedagogy by which most college students learn and explain history. But if the data show that CEO performance isn't persistent, or if the résumé characteristics we commonly associate with quality don't, in fact, predict performance, are investors making a mistake in spending so much time on management quality?[12]

Since 1987, this one-in-five ratio has barely moved. In 2024, only 22 percent of Fortune 1,000 CEOs had an MBA.[13] In 2018, the *Washington Post* reported that CEOs with engineering degrees had surpassed those with MBAs in *Harvard Business Review*'s annual one hundred best-performing CEOs in the world list.[14]

Scholars have attempted to more carefully assess the benefits of the MBA degree. A 2006 study by Gottesman and Morey found that (1) CEOs with an MBA or law degree performed no better than a CEO with no graduate degree, (2) CEOs who graduate from more prestigious schools do no better than those who graduate from less prestigious schools, (3) CEOs with a graduate degree in something other than business administration or law had "slightly better risk-adjusted market performance than other firms," and (4) that CEOs who graduated from more prestigious schools were paid more.[15]

A 2010 study by Bhagat, Bolton, and Subramanian concluded that "while CEO education appears to play an important role in the hiring of CEOs, it does not affect the long-term performance of firms."[16] Another study, published in 2015, similarly concluded that "there is no strong evidence of a relationship between CEO education and firm performance, while there is weak—and, perhaps, statistically insignificant—evidence that the leadership of a CEO from Top 100 companies having an MBA degree enables better operating performance. There is no consistent, long-term relationship between [a] CEO's MBA and firm performance."[17]

In other words, an MBA can help an individual get a job, but the training that MBA programs provide doesn't actually give the hiring company a leg up on the competition. Rasmussen and Li cut the data every which way and concluded, "MBA programs simply do not produce CEOs who are better at running companies, if performance is measured by stock price return."[18]

For an education curriculum specifically designed to understand and improve firm performance, this is a pretty terrible track record.

But it may be worse than this. In fact, studies have found mounting evidence that MBA-holding leaders may perform *worse* than their peers in several key respects.

A 2016 study by Miller and Xu found that MBA-grad CEOs pursue growth through acquisitions rather than organic growth and, consequently, grow slower and decline faster than companies led by a CEO without an MBA.[19] A follow-up study the next year by the same team found that "MBA CEOs are more apt than their non-MBA counterparts to engage in short-term strategic expedients such as positive earnings management and suppression of R&D, which in turn are followed by compromised firm market valuations."[20]

Miller and Xu attribute these results to self-serving behavior, which they think must somehow be instilled or nurtured by MBA programs—an unlikely explanation. We attribute it to *administration.*

In 1990, David Ewing published a book entitled *Inside the Harvard Business School*, which effused praise on the school. One particular piece of evidence was a list of nineteen HBS alumni who "had made it to the top." Henry Mintzberg and Joseph Lampel followed up on this list a decade later. How were those top-performing MBAs doing?

> In a word, badly. A majority, 10, seemed clearly to have failed, meaning that their company went bankrupt, they were forced out of the CEO chair, a major merger backfired, and so on. The performance of another 4 we found to be questionable. Some of these 14 CEOs built up or turned around businesses, prominently and dramatically, only to see them weaken or collapse just as dramatically.[21]

There is one industry where the evidence points the other way, where MBA-holding leaders outperform their peers: banks.[22] But it's easy enough to see why. Banks are one of the excessively few industries, replete with industry rules and regulations, where administration tends to be quite effective. Another would be logistics, although we will challenge even that one shortly.

The evidence points very clearly to a conclusion that MBAs offer an individual a leg upward on the corporate ladder, but it makes their holders no better an executive and may actually contribute to worse corporate performance. Why? Because MBAs are trained in administration, not entrepreneurial leadership.

The MBA Is Not Needed

Many of the world's top CEOs never finished college: Larry Ellison, Steve Jobs, Bill Gates, Mark Zuckerberg, Richard Branson, John Mackey, and the list goes on. A notably surprising number of successful tech founders dropped out of school to found a company. Very few of these top execs run their companies as administrators. They never had it drubbed into them.

There may be a selection effect here that we should admit to. It may be that people inclined toward administration—people who think the MBA way of doing business is the right way to do business—are the ones who pursue the degree. Perhaps. In our experience, most people who pursue an MBA aren't really familiar enough with the curriculum, or with the philosophy of science, to know one way or another. But *we* do know the curriculum. It's administration through and through. We'll go into some of the details of it in later chapters.

But let's conclude this chapter with a quick story.

Chang Yun Chung (also known as Teo Woon Tiong), who died in 2020 at the ripe age of 102, was the founder of Singaporean entrepôt industry giant Pacific International Lines. Chung started the company in 1967 with a mere two secondhand ships and grew it into a top *twenty* shipping company with eighteen thousand employees.

He was almost one hundred when he finally passed the baton of leadership to his son, Teo Siong Seng. And yet, even after the hand-off of responsibility, he couldn't help himself—he still would go to the office every day to check in on things. He loved his company.

Chang Yun Chung understood that business leadership is not administration. It's not about mergers and acquisitions, crunching numbers, or looking over shoulders.

Teo recounted his father's wisdom: "My father taught me one thing: In Chinese, it's 'yi de fu ren'—that means you want people to obey you not because of your authority, not because of your power, or because you are fierce, but more because of your integrity, your quality, that people actually respect you and listen to you."[23]

In other words, *yi de fu ren* is *entrepreneurial leadership*—it's about vision, passion, and grit. Success is achieved in venture mode. And it's on the rise.

PART II
THE PRESENT

CHAPTER 4

THE RISE OF VENTURE MODE

The purpose of business is human thriving. Its product is human well-being, which occurs when needs are satisfied, and people have a feeling of betterment and improvement. We call this proposition *value creation.*

The engine for value creation is entrepreneurship, which is the economic process of identifying needs that are yet unmet, designing and producing creative and innovative solutions to meet them, and providing those solutions to customers. Entrepreneurship is often mistakenly associated solely with start-ups and small businesses, but according to entrepreneurship theory, it's actually much broader and much more (economically) fundamental.

Entrepreneurship is the performance of the *function* of value creation. In other words, any time we aim to create new value, we're acting as an entrepreneur, just as anytime we're employing or expending resources to realize (i.e., experience) the value created, we're acting as a consumer. But note that by "create new value," we don't mean any production activity. Most of our production activities are not efforts to create *new* value but are aimed at replicating *familiar* value—they're *administrative* rather than *entrepreneurial*. But when we try something new, to innovate and deviate from normal value patterns, we're acting entrepreneurially.

Entrepreneurship is the driving force of the economy, the energy of innovative action, and a culture of pursuing value. When a firm harnesses these, it's in venture mode.

In this chapter and the next, we'll unpack these core functional differences in terms of the way businesses operate.

THE CONCEPT OF VENTURE MODE

Entrepreneurial business is conducted in venture mode—the commitment of capital (financial, physical, digital, intellectual, and human), arrayed in unique and novel configurations to facilitate new customer well-being. Capital has to be committed under conditions of uncertainty—venturers can't be certain if they'll be successful in the marketplace. They have to commit to investment in the here and now, knowing that any potential return on invested capital could be well into the future, and may never come. Therefore, venture mode is ambitious, adventurous, and innovative. It isn't content with current value propositions. New value creation is its sole aim and purpose. Administrative bureaucracy isn't allowed to get in the way.

The term *venture mode* is more universally applicable than the original *founder mode*, which connotes a sort of Silicon Valley exceptionalism. *Founder mode* implies, or at least connotes, that it's necessary for the founder to still be around. *Venture mode* doesn't. In fact, Brian Chesky, CEO of Airbnb and originator of the *founder mode* concept, specifically endorsed this broader idea:

> By the way, you don't need to be a founder to [be in founder mode]. You can apply founder mode to government, you can apply founder mode to a nonprofit, to a volunteer organization, to being a sports coach. It just means the leadership is present in the details, and it's not about being so-called autocratic because you're not telling the experts what to do.[1]

But both terms—*founder mode* and our preferred *venture mode*—express a clear focus on creating value (i.e., greater well-being) through entrepreneurship. As we'll examine in chapter five, venture mode has an identifiable set of characteristics that contribute to the increases in economic well-being we all seek. In fact, entrepreneurial economists (those who follow the Austrian school of economics) recognize that entrepreneurship (both new venturing and corporate entrepreneurship) drives the market, makes it grow, keeps it dynamic, sparks innovations, and creates jobs.

But venture mode can't emerge or succeed if it's dragged down by administration. The difference lies in the logic of control versus the philosophy of freedom.

Administration mode was born out of the desire for control. When Frederick W. Taylor wrote the first management handbook—*The Principles of Scientific Management*, referenced in the prior chapter—he laid down the first management control framework. The goal was to manage every individual worker to achieve the same targeted level of productivity.

His primary tool was the time-and-motion study, which measured how long it took the best worker to perform one unit of work (like shoveling coal). This best performance level would become the benchmark for the scientific manager, who would then coerce every other worker to achieve the same level of productivity or else be replaced with someone who could.

The result was called *efficiency*, which is still what administrators aim for today. Famously, Taylor remarked, "In the past, the man has been first; in the future the system must be first."[2] Remember this quote when you hear the term *management systems*—they can be antihuman.

There have been many management consultants, gurus, advisors, and professors since Taylor, and almost all follow some version of a control logic—that is, administration mode. They advise and assist managers in their aim to control outcomes (e.g., via managed earnings to control the numbers for Wall Street analysts' consumption), to mitigate variability (via "planning"), to control people (which is the origin of the HR department), or to control perceptions (the PR department).

Control is exercised through hierarchical authority (i.e., managers telling others what to do) and what business schools call processes and methods (i.e., telling others how to do it). In management lingo, firms are engineered (or reengineered) to operate their processes and methods efficiently, following guidelines like Lean or Six Sigma. There's little conceptual distance between these techniques and Taylor's.

In stark contrast, venture mode has no control logic. Instead, it leverages the advantages of *freedom*.

Freedom is the energy for economic thriving at every level, leveraging the energy of self-interest. In other words, it takes advantage of the fact that virtually everyone wants and is motivated by the prospect of a better life. At a national level, economic freedom, as defined by the Fraser Institute, means individuals and businesses have the ability to make their own choices—what to produce, consume, and trade—within a framework of stable property rights, low taxes, and minimal government interference.[3] This environment fosters innovation, incentivizes investment, and allows for efficient allocation of resources. When entrepreneurs and firms face fewer barriers, they can respond to market demands and capitalize on opportunities, creating jobs and driving economic growth.[4]

Vast empirical evidence supports this theory. The correlation between economic freedom and economic productivity is one of the starkest and clearest in all of the social sciences.[5] The reason for this, scholars have pointed out, is that freedom unleashes more, and more productive, entrepreneurship—the wellspring of economic growth.[6]

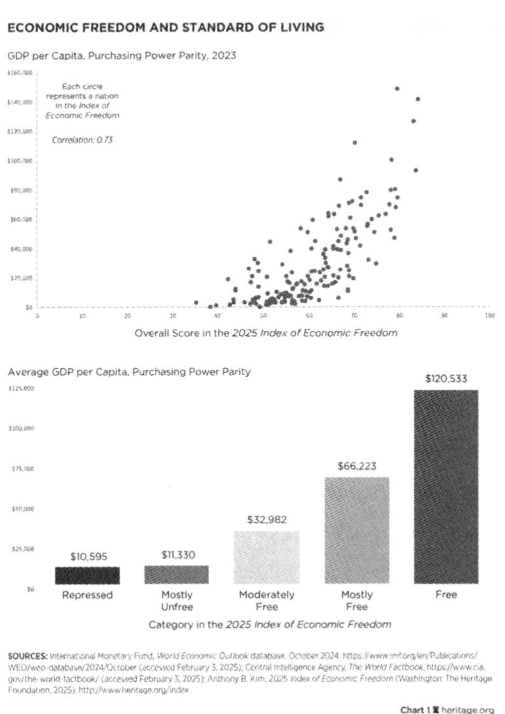

Source: Used with permission from The Heritage Foundation, The Index of Economic Freedom, 2025. www.heritage.org/index/pages/report.

At the level of the firm, giving employees greater autonomy—freedom to make decisions, experiment, and innovate—generally leads to stronger collaboration, faster problem-solving, and ultimately, better business outcomes.[7] In other words, increasing freedom by loosening the grip of bureaucracy and rigid hierarchies can unleash a firm's full entrepreneurial potential.

Research shows that firms with higher levels of employee autonomy experience stronger engagement, reduced turnover, and more robust innovation pipelines. Employees given the freedom to think creatively and take calculated risks are more likely to generate ideas that drive revenue growth or cut costs. A *Harvard Business Review* study on self-managed teams found that such approaches also improve agility, enabling firms to respond to market changes more quickly.[8]

At the individual level, freedom is the key to unlocking human potential, creativity, and fulfillment. Psychologists and thinkers like Edward Deci, Richard Ryan, Mihaly Csikszentmihalyi, Daniel Pink, and many others have highlighted how autonomy enables people to perform at their best, not just for personal satisfaction but also as valuable contributors to broader progress and improvement.

Venture mode harnesses the power of freedom and focuses in on creating value for customers. It doesn't aim to control anything. It seeks to understand customers through the lens of empathy rather than data, discovering what they value most, creating and designing new offerings for their approval, and responding to the feedback they provide when they buy or don't buy. As such, it's dynamic, responsive, and evolutionary. Venture mode succeeds by empathizing, learning, and adapting, not by controlling or managing.

EXAMPLES OF VENTURE MODE

While all founders are entrepreneurs, not all entrepreneurs are founders. In fact, one need not even be a business leader to operate in venture mode. Venture mode is a *mindset*, an approach to economic production that actively looks for new needs and new solutions rather than simply streamlining how it's always been done.

Productivity can increase with more efficient work, but this approach quickly reaches an upper bound, past which there are no additional gains. Being the most efficient in an industry can beat competitors. *But it can't beat innovators.*

Continued, long-term growth, then, requires entrepreneurship—shifting production activities to new and better solutions rather than recreating the same familiar value propositions over and over again. Firms that don't operate in venture mode often gain in the short term but inevitably fall behind and eventually fail due to an inability to keep up with disruptions to their industry.

Yet, administration mode is far more dominant in business than venture mode. Short-termism dominates strategic management because, without the short-term efficiency gains of administration mode's streamlining efforts, the more efficient competition starts to win. We get it. Venture mode is risky. But there are multiple examples of businesses of all sizes that have been able to maintain venture mode, especially in times of significant change, when administrative control tends to be an impediment. We will highlight four: Tesla, Morning Star, Haier, and Handu.

Big Business in Venture Mode: Tesla

Tesla CEO Elon Musk doesn't have an MBA, although he holds degrees in both economics and physics. Unencumbered by a traditional business management education, he's guided several companies to outstanding levels of achievement. Tesla, for example, generated just under $100 billion in revenues in 2024, with a market capitalization of just under $1.5 trillion. The company is well known for its continuous innovation.

Ending the Traditional Management Hierarchy

Under Musk's leadership, Tesla maintains a relatively flat structure, curtailing the traditional middle manager role, minimizing bureaucracy, and fostering direct communication. There's no company ladder to climb, no career planning, no promotions. This approach contrasts with traditional hierarchical models, facilitating collaboration, speed, and a more agile response to challenges.

Teams form the unit of organization, and they're configured dynamically. They're short-lived, cross-functional, and composed for specific tasks or projects. This flexibility ensures that the right expertise is applied precisely where needed rather than locked into departmental silos or inflexible roles. And it fosters collaboration and innovation.

There may well be moments of decision-making where individuals step into leadership roles because they have the right knowledge or experience to solve a specific problem at a specific time and in a specific context. Yet these roles rotate: Different individuals perform them at different times. In venture mode, anyone and everyone can be a leader—leadership is distributed and situational.

Compensation levels are also kept as flat as possible. People who work at Tesla are encouraged to purchase stock so that the company's success driven by high performance rewards everyone.

Speed over Process

Tesla places great emphasis on rapid, relevant information to empower individuals and teams and resolve problems and blockages. The goal is simple: Provide easy access to meaningful information in an understandable and practical way to enable employees to make fast, informed, and sound decisions over their respective responsibilities. Humans—not process templates—are the arbiters of what's creatively useful. Specific teams are responsible for keeping the information library updated quickly so that teams always have the current working version of production systems.

They have very few meetings. Teams often form and reform spontaneously over a period of three or four hours. There's no administrative organization process—no process map could cope with the swirl of change. There's no design process, just a current design that is in production. Design never stops—it's constant.

Also, there's no formal budgeting process. Budgeting is replaced by real-time monitoring of spend, burn, the pool of money, cost of production, and capital efficiency. Everyone in the company benefits from autonomous access to resources, which eliminates all barriers to speedy implementation.

Customer Value Is the Key Driver

Short-term accounting profit is not what wins the game, according to Musk. Long-term value creation is the goal. Profit is useful and good, and it is 100 percent reinvested in future innovation. Creating more and more customer value over time is the single-minded purpose of venture mode.

For instance, Musk's master plan was to build a superior electric car targeted at and priced for affluent, green-conscious users who valued the early opportunity and were comfortable in the market vanguard. The proceeds from this beachhead market were then recycled to build a less expensive electric car to provide value for a broader swath of sustainability-conscious users.

The proceeds from that were then used to build an affordable electric car that broadened the market even further, one valued not only for sustainability but also for everyday functionality. Over time, and from all these users, Tesla collected and processed more and more data, making the user experience more and more valuable and enabling software innovations that could be downloaded directly to customer vehicles.

The Tesla battery technology, charging system, and direct-to-consumer software system are all directed toward an enhanced user experience. Customer value compounds over time.

Profitability is the outcome, not the driver, of the Tesla business model.

Tesla and the MBA

Marc Andreessen, cofounder of Netscape and Opsware and current venture fund founder who has worked closely with Elon Musk, compared Musk's highly successful management approach with the traditional management skills taught in business school:

> Most large companies are not run by engineers. They're run by trained business people. There is a real challenge there. . . . It's just the way that management is taught. And most classically in the form of something like a Harvard Business School or Stanford Business School. . . . It's basically management as it was sort of developed and implemented, I would say in the 1950s, '60s, '70s . . . the so-called scientific school of management. It's basically management as a generic skill that you can apply to any industry and you can manage a soup company or you can manage a, I don't know, whatever kind of company, and they're kind of all the same, and it kind of doesn't matter what they do. And there's a common set of management practices, and it has a lot to do with process. How do you structure? How do you manage the balance sheet? How do you set the review schedule for the meetings? How do you do compliance? How do you hire and motivate executives?

> How do you resolve interpersonal conflicts? All these general business skills.
>
> That training gives you none of what you need to go do what Elon does. And then Elon, I would say he pushes it as far as he can and not doing all the stuff that you're classically trained to do so that he can spend all of his time doing the things that only he can do.

Andreessen added:

> [While] most other large companies are still having the planning meeting for the pre-planning meeting, for the board meeting, for the presentation for this, with the compliance review and the legal review, Elon shows up every week at each of his companies. He identifies the biggest problem that the company's having that week, and he fixes it. And then he does that every week for fifty-two weeks in a row. And then each of his companies has solved the fifty-two biggest problems that year in that year.

He then compared Musk to other business titans—many of whom existed before there were any business schools—who also ran their businesses in venture mode:

> The industrialists of the late 1800s, early 1900s, people like Henry Ford or Andrew Carnegie or Thomas Watson who built IBM, if you go back and read the biographies of people like that, Andrew Mellon, Cornelius Vanderbilt, those guys ran very similar to the way that Elon runs things. The top-line thing is just this incredible devotion from the leader of the company to fully deeply understand

> what the company does and to be completely knowledgeable about every aspect of it, and to be in the trenches and talking directly to the people who do the work, deeply understanding the issues and being the lead problem solver in the organization.[9]

The Medium-Sized Business in Entrepreneur Mode: The Morning Star Company

Christopher Rufer founded The Morning Star Company, a tomato-processing company that today is number one in its field, profitably generating over $1 billion in revenue and growing vigorously.

The secret to Morning Star's success? Instead of thinking from the perspective of alternative organizational design for his new company, Rufer started from first principles. There were two:

1. There was to be no use of coercion in interpersonal relations and interactions in the company.
2. Every colleague would keep their commitments to others and always do what they say they would do.

Whereas the foundational principle of management is command authority based on position, title, or decision rights, Rufer insisted that these two principles were to constitute the entirety of the governance of The Morning Star Company. This simple governance framework enabled Morning Star to stay permanently in venture mode.

The term that Rufer used for this new approach was "self-management," a term Jobs had also used (in chapter two). There was "no employee handbook and no giant rule book, no supervisors, no managers, no coordinators, no vice presidents, no titles of any kind."[10]

There were also no employees. Every individual was designated as a *colleague*, an elevation of status and an indicator of professionalism.

An Operating System for Individual Autonomy

While MBA programs will pay homage to employee autonomy, the management curriculum instills fear that self-management will lead to chaos—it's too uncontrolled in a paradigm of control. But Rufer was able to establish an operating system for individual autonomy. This operating system combines the first and second Morning Star principles (no coercion, always keep commitments) in a written peer agreement statement called the Colleague Letter of Understanding, or CLOU. These peer agreements are central to the concept of self-management, replacing the bureaucratic mechanisms of control and the politics of power positions with the integrity and trust of voluntary interpersonal commitment.

The CLOU is an accountability agreement between colleagues declaring each individual's personal commercial mission (why I work here), business process responsibilities (what I commit to do), scope of decision authority (what we both commit that I can decide), and performance measures (what I commit to deliver). CLOUs are trust agreements that are negotiated, not imposed. These commitments provide all the structure The Morning Star Company needs.

Replacing the Organization Chart

Traditional management generates an organizational chart with boxes, tiers, titles, and lines of reporting, visually representing the command-and-control mindset. Each box symbolizes an individual's role and authority, with vertical lines reflecting the flow of orders from the top down, reinforcing a clear chain of command. The rigid structure implies that decision-making power is concentrated at the top, while workers at lower levels are tasked primarily with executing instructions.

This framework emphasizes control, compliance, and uniformity, leaving little room for autonomy or decentralized decision-making.

The Morning Star Company, however, has never had an organizational chart. Since the operating system for individual autonomy is based on CLOUs, there's no purpose for such a depiction of power relationships. The organizational form is a three-dimensional dynamic network. People are free to enter or leave at any point, and the adaptation takes place without any command authority. This freedom is a key characteristic of venture mode.

A Big Business That Converted to Venture Mode: Haier

One of the most direct challenges to the traditional command-and-control hierarchy of business administration is the case of Haier, originally a Chinese manufacturer of household appliances and now a multilayered global assembly of end user experience ecosystems.

Haier converted from a company that manufactured products to a platform that incubated entrepreneurial ventures, replacing departments with self-organized microenterprises, eliminating over twelve thousand middle managers in the process.

Haier CEO Zhang Ruimin is quoted as saying,

> A company is full of energy when it is small, but as it grows bigger, there will be more and more layers in the organizational structure, making the wall between the company and its customers thicker and thicker. The company gets more bureaucratic. . . . Employees do not know where users are. A finance staff is satisfied with receiving budget reports regularly. A production worker is only responsible for working on the production line. "Why do I need to care about users? I just do what my supervisor asks me to do."[11]

Zhang set out to break the bureaucracy. His Rendanheyi model is a venture-launching and venture-sustaining platform rather than a structure. The first element of his vision is the user experience, and he specifically refers to users (the "dan" in Rendanheyi) as distinct from customers.

A customer may be viewed in the context of a transaction, whereas a user is seen through the lenses of continuous interaction and participation in the experience design and experience improvement process. Thus, users are considered lifelong friends and close partners of all platform participants.

The second element of the vision is the microenterprise, a small and autonomous unit that follows market rules and, according to Zhang, works to satisfy "their desires via their own efforts, instead of expecting the company to satisfy them."

The third element is the employee turned venturer. Employees have the autonomy to know who their users are and to create value for them. Haier demonstrates a foundational belief in liberating the entrepreneurial talents of their employees as the driving force of company success.

The Rendanheyi ecosystem is intended to be interconnected through continuous interaction with user communities. Microventures engage with users throughout the entire value creation process, from product design, through production and delivery, to the in-use experience. Through continuous interaction, microenterprises can encourage a population of lifetime users.

Haier provides initial venture funding to microenterprises, as well as other resources (such as R&D services, purchasing, distribution, and the service network). In traditional business lines, Haier is sometimes the largest shareholder of the microenterprises. The microenterprises can raise funds from outside investors. Haier approves "user value creation" targets, a blend of financial and nonfinancial metrics tracked through a win-win value added (WWVA) statement. The targets can include the following:

- **User-centric innovation:** This includes products, services, or solutions that address specific user pain points or preferences. The target here is often tied to metrics like user adoption rates or positive feedback.
- **Revenue growth:** End user value translates into willingness to pay, so revenue growth is a venture mode target. Each microventure must generate its own revenue by competing in a "value war," meaning they aim to maximize income by offering superior value.
- **Ecosystem value sharing:** Created value is shared among users, partner firms, the microventure team, and Haier itself. A key target is to build an ecosystem where ongoing user engagement generates recurring value. This might be measured by the number of "lifetime users" or the percentage of revenue from ecosystem services.
- **Nonfinancial user metrics:** The WWVA statement tracks metrics like the number of interactive users (those engaging with the microenterprise), active users (those regularly using its offerings), user interactions (frequency of engagement), and lifetime users (long-term customers).
- **Market opportunity capture:** Successful microenterprises are expected to identify and seize new market opportunities. The target here is often qualitative—create a new market segment—but gets quantified through sales or market share growth.
- **Self-sustainability and scalability:** Microenterprises must meet performance thresholds to remain operational, such as securing venture funding or spinning off as independent entities with Haier as an investor.

Microenterprise founders set goals of market position and strategic pathways for their microenterprises and provide incubation and growth driver services, such as the Haier brand umbrella and distribution. They set the percentage of profits that the microenterprise owners can retain. These microenterprises aim to be the leading player in their industry with high value, high market share, and high profitability. They cultivate their user community in order to develop lifetime relationships and develop new revenue sources through new products and services.

Haier's approach contrasts with traditional corporate goals by tying compensation and survival directly to these outcomes—employees' pay reflects the value they create, and failing to meet targets can result in dissolving the microenterprise. It's a high-stakes entrepreneurial setup designed to keep Haier agile and innovative, even as a $40 billion global giant.

Haier represents a complete repudiation of the tradition of building a structure of layers of employees working in divided functions to achieve objectives set for them by those higher up in the hierarchy. Instead of a structure, Haier aims for an ecosystem of shared knowledge, shared resources, and shared relationships. Instead of vertical layers, Haier aims for a decentralized network of small, autonomous teams. Instead of a linear management structure of orders passed from the top down, Haier adapts to nonlinear processes in which employees respond adaptively to changes in the market.

Instead of employees, Haier nurtures entrepreneurs and aims to empower everyone in the enterprise to function entrepreneurially. Instead of transacting with customers, Haier cultivates "zero distance" to users, meaning that users are an equal partner in innovation, service development, and quality control, as well as a lifelong economic subscriber. And instead of paying employees a guaranteed salary, Haier cultivates the idea of *pay by user*—that compensation comes from and corresponds to total customer value creation and user satisfaction.

Haier is an enterprise without boundaries. Its ecosystem approach replaces traditional value chains with communities of microenterprises that might include both Haier entrepreneurial microcompanies and third parties. All recognize they can create more value for customers by working together rather than competing as individual entities. Smart contracts keep them bound together while also enabling bidding for new tasks when the value to end users can be raised to a higher standard.

Venture Mode from the Outset: Handu

As we enter a new, digitally enabled era of business, entrepreneurs are realizing that digital systems can be better than management systems for harnessing human creativity and the empathic interaction of value proposition design and customer needs. We are seeing the emergence of new digital ecosystems where autonomy, not management, provides the direction.

The Chinese company Handu Group provides an example of such a digital ecosystem. Since its founding in 2006, Handu has shown significant financial growth, reaching over USD 2 billion in revenues. Initially targeting young, female, fashion shoppers, it has generated multiple sub-brands targeting different demographics, including men's fashion, children's wear, and middle-aged women's clothes. It has also become a B2B service platform, managing other companies' brands through its "management agency" business. To do this, it has developed an agile, data-driven, digitally enabled three-system model with broad applicability.

At Handu, autonomous teams operate within an internal entrepreneurship model, with direct access to corporate resources and capabilities. These teams self-organize around specific business opportunities without resorting to management intervention, permission, or control. A team has a minimum of three members: a designer in charge of product development; a web page specialist responsible for online portal design, display, and sales; and a product management specialist in charge of sourcing, production, inventory, and logistics.[12] In addition to these, new specialists can be recruited to add to team capabilities as marketplace results direct.

Teams are responsible for identifying customers, markets and business, and innovation opportunities. The team monitors customer needs and value experiences and autonomously adapts and expands product development, new product launches, discounts, and promotions. As products and sub-brands are added, teams are free to add upstream and downstream partners (e.g., specialized suppliers) to the ecosystem for customized production and distribution.

There are shared success indicators that guide all teams (such as sales, gross profit, and inventory turns), but each team behaves independently in response to these indicators. Handu has made an indicator dashboard visible to all teams in real time so that internal peer emulation norms evolve as a catalyst for achieving better and better results. When the indicator dashboard shows subpar results, declines, or losses, the failing team may lose access to resources or even be closed down, its members transferred to new teams or new roles.

In venture mode, it's equally as important to reallocate investments *away* from failing value propositions as it is to find and fuel successful propositions.

Horizontally Linked Systems

In contrast to the traditional, "tall" hierarchical structures, teams in Handu's digital ecosystem are organized horizontally. They're directly connected to their customers, partners, and suppliers via Handu's digital commerce platforms, which constitute the front end of the horizontal structure. At the back end are the capital assets needed to support value flow to the customer: production plants, warehouses, computing hardware, and critical digital assets such as databases, including five hundred different curated fan groups who produce billions of impressions annually.[13]

Instead of middle management, Handu has developed a middle layer of software systems to link the front and back ends, organizing shared services, data, analytics, reporting, and the capabilities to assist front-end teams in their rapid, permissionless decision-making.

This software provides dynamic and adaptive capabilities for channeling demand, managing the supply chain, utilizing capital, and enabling the value experience. These middle-layer systems include business intelligence, warehouse management, transport management, supply chain management, supplier regulation management, and so on. Every team can access the software and data they need through the same platform, which also keeps track of project activities, progress, and results.

Handu's Efficiency in Venture Mode

Another benefit of Handu's autonomous team organization is the faster execution and decision-making that emerges from smaller teams needing narrow and clearly defined tasks, timelines, and budgets. Teams at Handu are highly focused on their own customers, their own website, their own line of products, and their own indicators. No distractions are brought on by central planning requirements, internal processes, meetings with management, or any of the usual bureaucratic impediments. Teams are compensated based on their own performance, with clear benchmarks to guide them. And internal systems are designed to enable these teams to be highly responsive to market feedback.

THE BEGINNING OF THE INEVITABLE SHIFT TO VENTURE MODE

These four companies aren't the only ones we could point to as venture mode leaders, but they are pioneers. Elon Musk and Christopher Rufer are founder-entrepreneurs who have been very willing to break with convention. Zhang Ruimin was never a founder, but he's considered a radical with few peers in management. The Handu Group was digitally native from birth, one of the first.

They're all free from the strictures of business administration. That doesn't mean that they don't have solid accounting and transparent reporting. They adhere to all legal requirements, safety procedures, and compliance norms. They have HR departments, training, catering, and all the baseline functions and benefits of other corporations. The difference is that they operate on the logic of freedom rather than the logic of control. Freedom is more creative, more innovative, and less bureaucratic. Business administration inherently curtails freedom—freedom is too risky and uncontrollable from within administration mode.

The logic of control mistakes risk for uncertainty. Uncertainty is opportunity. Uncertainty rewards bold initiative. Uncertainty is the realm of creativity. Uncertainty is the realm of venture mode.

CHAPTER 5

THE PRINCIPLES OF VENTURE MODE

Tesla, Morning Star, Haier, and Handu appear to be quite different from each other in their approach. And that's the point. Companies that operate in venture mode do so from a set of principles unique to them, manifesting in different ways from those in administration mode, who instead standardize to industry norms. In venture mode, there is no standard way. It doesn't conform to any management handbook.

Yet, while each firm is idiosyncratic, it is possible to identify a set of principles followed, in whole or part, by venture mode companies. Unsurprisingly, these are the same core principles of successful entrepreneurship. They are:

- founder's intent
- consumer sovereignty
- value in experience
- empathy as a business skill

- entrepreneurial ethic
- differentiation through purpose
- qualitative not quantitative
- networks, not hierarchies
- action over strategy
- busting bureaucracy
- individualism and autonomy
- generative business models

FOUNDER'S INTENT

We agree with Paul Graham in his summary of Brian Chesky's insight: All firms originate from founders' intent. This intent provides the birthing energy for new venturing and imparts growth momentum from the start. Vision and mission are wrapped in founder's intent. There's an emotional drive and commitment to succeed but also the hardened realism of capital at risk. Combined, these elements guarantee that decisions will be rapid and precise in response to market data.

There's love for the firm that the founding team has created. The entrepreneurial ethic of serving others to improve their lives generally reaches its highest development in founders. There is pragmatic management of costs to provide service efficiently and profitably—no fluff. The colleagues and followers of the founder are steeped in the same vision and mission and totally united in their joint efforts to create value.

Even after founders depart (usually as a result of retirement or exit), firms in venture mode are able to maintain the founder's intent through founder-inspired entrepreneurial leadership. It's a critical continuity to preserve and sustain the unique market relevance of the firm. The next generation of the firm's leaders and managers, if nurtured in venture mode, can recite the original vision and mission with the same urgency and hunger as the original founders. There need be no loss of veracity or authenticity. The values of the founding team remain the values of all succeeding teams, who have embraced them, even as markets and competitive environments change.

Amazon after the departure of Jeff Bezos remains the same customer powerhouse, running on the same set of leadership principles that Bezos formulated to align the firm with a shared vision without a top-down decree from the original founder. Principles like "customer obsession," "learn and be curious," and all the others that Bezos originated can guide a succession team for the long term.[1] And Amazon continues to grow in new business areas from cloud computing to cybersecurity and video production and distribution. In venture mode, the founder's intent supports forward momentum and counteracts any slide into administration mode.

CONSUMER SOVEREIGNTY

The defining insight of venture mode is to focus on the role of the end user in the economic system—what Amazon calls *customer obsession* and Austrian economics terms *consumer sovereignty*. The output of all economic activity is well-being for the population.[2] As Bezos put it, "It's our job every day to make every important aspect of the customer experience a little bit better."[3] Well-being is a dynamic feeling of circumstances improving. It's subjective, of course—each individual in the economy decides for themselves the quality of their circumstances, the prospects for improvement, and what they'll buy to bring about that improvement.

Traditional business economics views the end user as a customer, a recipient of production output, a consumer. Venture mode reverses this thinking. The end user is the *originator* in the economic process, the initiator of innovation. They provide all the causal energy for economic growth and the profitability of firms.

This is, in economics, called the principle of *consumer sovereignty*, which says that producers are beholden to their masters, i.e., consumers. It is consumers, end users, who are at the helm of the economy. End users assert themselves in this role by demanding their own well-being. They expect more, and they are never satisfied with their current situation, always imagining a better one and seeking to find it. That's the meaning of the term "consumer demand."

Consider the iPhone. Consumers didn't invent it and couldn't even conceive of it. Mobile phones are an enormously important human invention, offering breakthrough interconnectivity and interaction between people and opening up expansive new vistas and opportunities. What was the role of end users? They brought their dissatisfaction to bear.

End users had been offered mobile phones since the 1970s and 1980s, but early mobile phones were too big, too clunky, too expensive, and too limited in their use. End users demanded more. An inventor might be offended by their lack of gratitude, but the venture mode firm recognizes a pathway to the future illuminated by the end users' insistence on making it better.

What followed was the result of the end user genius of unrelenting insistence on improvement. The first generation of mobile networks was followed in the 1990s by the second—2G—with 3G in 2001, 4G in the 2010s, and 5G today. As the network generations evolved, they supported better and better handset functionality. First came feature phones with custom-designed software to support some internet capabilities, then smartphones with a CPU and all the advanced interconnectivity to support video, data, messaging, gaming, e-commerce, and a vast array of apps.

This all happens because the end user is never fully satisfied. They're always seeking new and better ways to use the handset and the network.

When his classes talk about the AI frontier and what it means for people at work, Mark frequently asks them, "When will there be no more scope for entrepreneurship?" The answer is, essentially, *never.* Mark has, in his research, called it the "Nirvana state of rest,"[4] the point at which all end users are perfectly and perpetually in a state of euphoric bliss. Until then, there will *always* be more entrepreneurial work to do and consumers to better satisfy, and we will continue to create new jobs to better serve each other. "Bring on the robots!" is often Mark's conclusionary remark to this class discussion.

Soon, end users will be coding their own apps using AI and a voice interface. The end user as initiator will enter a new phase. Apple is a good example of a venture mode firm that appreciates and anticipates evolving end user requirements, adding new chips and Apple Intelligence to their handsets and software that can facilitate as-yet-unknown future end user demands.

In venture mode, firms don't mistake invention for innovation. Innovation is what end users initiate. The role of firms in venture mode is to facilitate this end user–led process. Venture mode firms innovate successfully by putting the most demanding end users in charge and following their lead.

VALUE IN EXPERIENCE

The foundation for all venture mode firms is their concept of value.

Value creation is the singular purpose of all venture mode firms. The primary value, which takes precedence over all other claims to resources and effort, is specifically customer value—not stakeholder value or stock market value. Venture mode firms understand that value is fundamentally *subjective*, a perception that lies entirely in the minds of customers.

To elaborate somewhat, value is an experience for customers—experiencing that sense of well-being, feeling that their circumstances are improving as a result of their patronage of the firm. They're experiencing more comfort, more joy, more efficiency, more functionality, or more bang for the buck than would otherwise be the case. This experienced benefit, an increase in their well-being, renders them satisfied—pleased with the company or brand that helped them in improving their life. They are continuously making value judgments regarding the options they're offered in order to satisfy a particular felt need.

They specifically make value *comparisons* with the experience they expect to have with alternative choices—either real or projected—in order to make their value decisions. They're always evaluating. Value is a verb, not a noun; a process, not a thing.

End users ultimately express their value preference through willingness to pay—a sale is made—and they become customers. In this way, revenue generation is one of the ways venture mode firms can assess their capacity to facilitate value. However, the primary task is not to make money but to engender increased well-being and the feelings of satisfaction that accompany it. This is sometimes called "improving lives," which is perfectly valid. The customer's life is better for having the firm's products and services available.

As a result, making money follows, and the firm is tasked with establishing a cost structure to deliver customer value at a profit, which is necessary to sustain the business. Once this formula is established and proven, value can scale by increasing the well-being of more and more customers.

But value experiences are not just for end users; they're multidimensional. Venture mode companies were the first to understand the economic significance of *multidirectional* value. They understand how hard it is to deliver top-value experiences for customers if the team is dissatisfied. It turns out that colleagues and employees who experience value themselves are better at facilitating value for customers. Value experiences for colleagues are often identified as involving purpose, autonomy, and mastery:

- **Purpose** is found in job tasks and professional responsibilities that are felt to be a challenging and fulfilling use of skills and capabilities while contributing to the higher-level mission of increasing end user well-being.
- **Autonomy** is the feeling of freedom to make decisions and direct one's own responsibility.
- **Mastery** is the experience of getting better and better at using one's skills to the point of expertise and recognition.

Firms in venture mode recognize the value of these experiences for everyone on the payroll, with a clear view of the enhanced, and therefore profitable, end result for customers. It's captured in another of Bezos's principles: *hire and develop the best.*

There are additional value experiences for employees and colleagues, including security, collaboration, achievement, and team camaraderie. They're all available in venture mode.

And the value facilitation extends further to contract partners and contract negotiation, channel partners who provide distribution, outside service providers, agencies, and independent vendors, all of whom are included in venture mode's tuning of the ecosystem.

In venture mode, firms internalize the mindset that customers draw value from the firm to themselves. Venture mode firms humbly submit to the decisions of the end user.

The value mindset—to create end user value as a first priority with the confidence that revenue and profits will follow—is foundational for venture mode. Extending value in all directions beyond the firm itself strengthens the end user value proposition. This value mindset is not captured in strategy or planning or business administration. It is captured in empathy.

EMPATHY AS A BUSINESS SKILL

To create a value experience for someone else requires empathy, a deep and sympathetic understanding of the customer's emotional reasons for evaluating one choice over another.

End users' assignment of value may or may not be rational, but it is not a monetary calculation so much as it is an act of imagination. Whether the customer knows it or not, the act of choosing is an act of imagining a better future.

Whether they are choosing an automobile or an apple, they're anticipating future benefits. The automobile will bring them speedy, efficient, and safe transportation, with some creature comforts thrown in. They can see themselves in a new car as they envision the future. The apple will be delicious, crisp, and refreshing. They will enjoy it, for sure. And it aligns with their health goals.

This act of imagination is actually quite complex. It's counterfactual in that the imagined future hasn't arrived yet—and it might never. It's definitely idiosyncratic, but most of all, it's *subjective*. Value is experienced subjectively, as is its imaginative prediction.

So how can venture mode marketers and product developers imagine what the customer would imagine and experience as valuable? Well, they can't, actually. But if they are good at empathy, they can simulate that imagination. Just as a video game simulates reality and a computer model simulates tomorrow's weather before it arrives, it is possible to simulate what another person might be experiencing or imagining.

How?

The mental model is a tool often used in science. An observer or researcher can construct a model of how others think, how they make choices, and the value assessment tools they use. Often, firms will do this through conversations with a small number of end users in which they answer questions about why they prefer one beer or one automobile or one software suite over another—and also, how they make decisions.

But Steve Jobs wasn't wrong when he observed that most people don't know what they want until you show it to them. So what good are research subjects who can't tell you anything?

Well, the secret to powerful entrepreneurial empathy is in *whom* you listen to, whom you bring into your focus groups. Most people say they just want what they like, what is familiar to them. That's not exactly right. They would certainly prefer something *better*, but they don't know what that is and are wary of blowing their money on untested alternatives.

So how does the venture mode company figure it out? How did Jobs?

Again, the trick is to talk to people who *don't* just want what they like, or what is familiar to them. It's to talk to people who desperately want something *better.*

We often call these people *lead users* because they're always at the cutting edge of a market, searching for the next new thing that might be better. These are the people who have imagined better. They might not have great solutions yet, but they will have ideas. And they understand the problems with current solutions better than anyone.

After finding and talking to lead users, venture researchers can construct a mental model of end users' decision trees. These mental models will never be perfectly accurate, but they can come close with practice. The researchers can follow up with a prototype offering designed to appeal to their mental model: Does the end user prefer the new product or not? End user behavior in the test will validate the accuracy of the mental model the researchers constructed.

Most importantly, this process is human-to-human. It's not the analysis of big data sets. It's more intuitive than it is hard science. Some individuals are more empathic than others. But empathy is a valid scientific method. It is the development of hypotheses about how an end user might feel about the possibility of a better future when presented with a new value proposition, which can then be tested in experimental validation. More importantly, empathy is a business skill that can be nurtured in venture mode through exploration and experience of others' feelings.

You can see this play out every day with the Netflix recommendation engine. Netflix asks users to give a thumbs up or thumbs down to their streaming content simply by clicking an icon. Thumbs up or thumbs down is an emotional evaluation. The user doesn't think that deeply about their rationale, they simply sum up their feelings in one click.

Netflix researchers analyze the patterns in the data, and they can then hyperpersonalize the configuration of content offerings to that user in a way that will empathically align with their expressed preferences. *We know you like this kind of content, and we think we understand why, so we're offering you this new selection.* There's an empathy engine running at Netflix.

ENTREPRENEURIAL ETHIC

In contemporary culture, business is often viewed as cold and exploitative, driven by the profit motive to exclude the warmth of human kindness. The opposite is true in venture mode. The value mindset and the empathic approach to customers combine to produce a specific and distinctive commitment to increasing end user well-being. We call it the *entrepreneurial ethic.*

The reason for conducting business is to make customers' lives better. Businesses can do this with empathy and understanding of how and why customers feel better as a result of using products and services. Those two characteristics—understanding and empathy—are the foundations of the entrepreneurial ethic. There is no room for exploitation, insincerity, overpromising, or under-delivery. These business behaviors lead to failure.

The service ethic is the business driver. This harkens back to the consumer sovereignty principle. The service is always an offering, or what is sometimes and rightly called a value proposition. The decision to accept it—or not—is always with the customer. Also, the evaluation of the experience after the service is used lies entirely in the customer's domain. Customers decide your success, and they will not choose you if you prove untrustworthy.

The entrepreneurial ethic is characterized by humility. Venture mode businesses never assume they know better than the user. Customers may not always be right, but success isn't really about being *right*—it's about understanding each other. If they aren't persuaded by your pitch, you need to learn from them. Clearly you don't understand their experience in the same way they do. You don't speak their language. So venture mode businesses adopt a process of learning from customers and markets rather than one of setting strategy and making plans.

The entrepreneurial ethic affects the attitude of the whole business at multiple levels. Teams within the firm can take inspiration and meaning from the work of improving customers' lives. Business partners can be motivated by contributing their ingredients or components to the customer value pie and earning their slice. And outside observers, especially young people who sometimes question the ethics of business and corporations, can be persuaded to rethink their negativity.

Service to others as the purpose of business activity is an elevating idea, rising above the anti-capitalist slogans of profiteering and exploitation. The entrepreneurial ethic has the potential to turn the negative public sentiment toward business institutions positive.

In a Gallup survey in 2024, only 6 percent of Americans reported having a "great deal" of confidence in big business.[5] There's a persistent skepticism to overcome. Some (maybe much) of this public skepticism has been rightly earned by businesses operating in administration mode, under an administration ethic. A clear and consistent demonstration of the entrepreneurial ethic can make a big difference.

DIFFERENTIATION THROUGH PURPOSE

With the entrepreneurial ethic as a minimum standard, individual businesses seek to find the part of the landscape where they can create even more value in customers' minds. This search for higher value is often referred to as differentiation: occupying a unique space of acceptance and approval in customers' minds.

Differentiation is based on two complementary components of venture mode. The first is entrepreneurial empathy—knowing and understanding a specific group of customers really well and better than any other firm, at least with regard to some particular need or problem. Knowledge and understanding go deeper than demographics and survey research, deeper than purchase records, email response rates, and digital marketing metrics.

Venture mode success results from a truly deep understanding of customers' *lives*. The relationship with customers is a whole-life relationship. Life is a system with multiple interconnecting channels and strands of behaviors, interactions, and cross-dependencies. This is as true of home life as it is of office life or factory life.

Doing business in venture mode means taking a deep interest in customers' lives and experiences and how differentiated solutions address their needs. This deep understanding not only demonstrates to customers that firms truly care about them, but it also engenders an ability to discover new ways to improve their lives, which brings us to the second component.

The second component is to creatively contribute something new to improve the system without disrupting it. Improving customers' lives involves making their life systems work better. This is *systems* thinking at a highly refined level: thinking of the future system and how it will evolve. Venture mode embraces an evolving purpose of continuously enhancing already functioning systems.

When a customer can discern that a particular firm's purpose is the improvement of their life system and that it has the unmatched idiosyncratic know-how to bring about that purpose, then high differentiation results.

Competition in venture mode is not "red in tooth and claw" as some would have it. It is entrepreneurial rivalry between firms to serve the end user in more and better ways, elevating all experiences and every firm's performance. Tesla and the EV market provide a telling example. All the firms involved in the EV ecosystem benefit from improving the electronic vehicle user experience, from driving to real-time data processing to charging. The electronic vehicle market gets better for all participants when all the participating manufacturers serve the end user with improved experiences.

QUALITATIVE, NOT QUANTITATIVE

Business thinking and business education are dominated by quantification. To "make the numbers" is the highest accolade for management. Everything must be measured, and what gets measured gets done. Both financialization—which promotes the expression of every business variable in dollars and cents—and digitization—which promotes dashboards and data charts and sliders for display purposes—have strongly influenced this mindset.

Financialization imposes quantitative targets from third-party analysts: quarterly earnings, returns on capital, operating ratios, subscriber growth targets, profit margins, free cash flow targets, and many, many more. These metrics are increasingly shortsighted, as metric horizons shrink from quarterly to monthly to weekly to daily.

Digitization has made the obsession with numbers even more intense, since many more business activities and results are measurable. You're probably familiar with many of these terms:

- page views
- click-throughs
- conversion ratios
- lifetime customer value
- cost of customer acquisition
- advertising performance by channel
- platform and individual website visits, by hour, minute, and second

Digital marketing has been especially destructive to the emotional connection between companies, their brands, and their consumers. How much love is the customer feeling? This is deemed irrelevant by today's marketers since they can't enumerate it. So instead, they pay attention only to the number of clicks. Today, marketers talk about engagement with customers and not about them falling in love with brands.

In venture mode, the fixation with numbers is tempered by a deeper understanding of the role of qualitative assessments such as

- customer insights
- emotional attachment

- levels of empathy
- personal values
- social ties
- perceptions
- preferences
- expectations

Qualities that can't be measured are the most important to building strong customer relationships and bonds of trust with employees and forging strong business partnerships. Venture mode businesses are at their best when they feel comfortable using qualitative assessments of the level of subjective value they generate.

How do you measure love? In venture mode, firms enter a love affair with their customers, nurturing a lasting two-way relationship of desire and fulfillment (although pragmatic economists use the terms *demand* and *supply*). Love is not quantifiable, but depth of affection can be felt by empathic marketers.

For instance, people really love their lululemon workout wear and their YETI coolers, so much so that they'll proudly display the brand logos on everything from wearables to bumper stickers. You can quantify these customers' buying behavior. You can survey their satisfaction. But it's impossible to put a valid number on how they feel.

NETWORKS, NOT HIERARCHIES

One of the greatest impediments to firms' creative and adaptive navigation of markets is the hierarchical structure of authority in traditional business administration models. Within these structures, every idea and action must be cleared by the level above. The goal is control, and the result is often slowness and delay, loss of customer and market insights, and dampened enthusiasm for initiative taking.

Venture mode emphasizes the network in place of the hierarchy because it gives more importance to interconnection than to authority. Information is free to flow from the customer and the market and between nodes in the internal network, irrespective of people's titles and roles. This flow of information is vital to entrepreneurial leaders and employees being "in the details," as Brian Chesky explained.[6] There's just too much information loss in a hierarchy's game of telephone to run effectively in venture mode.

Venture mode networks span the firm horizontally without divisional or functional demarcations and vertically insofar as there are any levels at all. The network is the organizational structure of venture mode firms, without boxes on org charts, differentiated titles, or power authority. Flow of knowledge and value is the driver of decision-making rather than the power or authority of position.

Amazon, for example, is a highly interconnected network of customers, partners, suppliers, and employees. Retailers can self-organize their online store on the Amazon platform and plug into the Fulfillment By Amazon (FBA) order fulfillment and delivery system.

If the retailer generates strong sales and good reviews, Amazon will promote their offerings more and reinforce the shared benefits of collaboration. Packing, shipping, returns, and customer service are handled by Amazon with feedback to the retailer. There are no hierarchies here and no "who does what" disputes. It's a flexible, multidirectional network based on discovery, not authority.

ACTION OVER STRATEGY

Strategy has long been one of the most prized elements of intellectual property in management science, and a business school with a reputation for excellence in the field of strategy gathers disproportionate prestige. But strategy is not nearly so important in venture mode for the simple reason that strategy is an attempt to predict and control, or at least to greatly influence, the future.

It can't be done, not in the long term. Firms may feel they can succeed in the short term with a good strategy, in the sense of "positioning" themselves well vis-à-vis their competitors. But a strategy like this can only work insofar as there is comparatively little entrepreneurship in the industry.

The venture mode mindset embraces the truth that the future is unpredictable, the result of billions and trillions of microinteractions between individuals, firms, markets, and institutions that can scarcely be monitored, let alone controlled.

Consequently, venture mode prioritizes *action* over strategy. Entrepreneurship is a process of exploration and discovery. Exploration can be guided by purpose—i.e., *do this for these specific customers, to enhance this specific benefit area*—but is primarily experimental: *Try this, try that.*

Tech companies often use the term A/B test, where A and B are alternative actions to achieve the benefit result, and their respective performances are experimentally compared so that a decision can be made regarding which action to take. There is no preference or judgment in favor of one versus the other. In venture mode, strategy is essentially replaced by A/B testing.

The feedback loop is integral to the action paradigm. Action occurs in the market with the customer's approval and selection in mind. The feedback loop is the customer's communication of their evaluation of an experience. A feedback loop can be transmitted through repeat purchase and loyalty or through choosing a competitive offering next time around.

The action-minded entrepreneurial business focuses on actual customer behaviors. The empathic entrepreneurial mind can deduce the customers' attitudes from their purchase behaviors without any need for surveys or secondary measures. Insofar as there is doubt or potential misunderstanding, these are resolved through conversations with customers rather than surveys.

BUSTING BUREAUCRACY

Bureaucracy is the enemy of entrepreneurial value creation. Bureaucracy is defined as action and associated allocated time where the primary purpose is not value creation for the customer but internal coordination and control. It exists in organizations for two reasons: (1) to standardize practices and processes and (2) to enable administrative control over the actions of subordinate roles in the firm. Venture mode rejects both reasons.

Standardization, while potentially a pathway to efficiency, represses creativity and innovation. As Ken Iverson said when he was CEO of Nucor Steel, "Forced standardization chokes off innovation and turns employees into automatons. [At Nucor] there are no attempts to impose uniformity merely for the sake of orderliness."[7]

Efficiency is a benefit to the firm in the form of greater output for the same or less input. But it is not necessarily a benefit for the customer unless the savings are passed on. The entrepreneurial employee who is closest to the customer may spot some nonstandard opportunity to adjust a service for a better fit with the customer system.

But if they are prevented from implementing efficiency as a violation of a bureaucratic standard, then this prohibitive bureaucracy deeply violates the responsiveness of venture mode. Venture mode prefers "permissionless innovation"[8]—adaptiveness and responsiveness without needing authorization from an administrator.

Worse still, administration mode can do actual harm to customers. Dr. Walter O'Donnell of Massachusetts General Hospital coined a term for it: *adminogenic harm*—harm caused to patients by administrative decisions and rules, not by clinical care.[9]

One instance given by Dr. O'Donnell was the cancellation due to budget cuts of a very successful (50–70 percent success rate) tobacco treatment program that helped smokers quit and was a necessary prerequisite for critical surgery. An administrative decision was made to cut the program for efficiency (i.e., cost-saving) reasons. Consequently, a patient who needed the surgery was precluded from receiving it because the pretreatment was no longer available.

Leading business consultant Michele Zanini tells us the problem of adminogenic harm permeates not only hospitals but all business organizations:

> It's the product innovation suffocated by a 15-signature approval process. It's the customer service rep who can't issue a $50 refund without three levels of approval. . . . It's the performance management system that measures everything except actual performance. This is the daily toll of bureaucracy, and it inflicts substantial damage"[10]

The bureaucracy of control is induced by the existence of hierarchical strata. Top executives and "chiefs" decide on policies and communicate them to senior, intermediate, and junior managers, so that they eventually reach the lower levels or "front lines" as mandates to be followed. This requires not only written communications in the form of handbooks and policy manuals but also digital administration in the form of templates and data fields to fill out.

And, most of all, it requires meetings. Many executive and managerial days are spent in back-to-back meetings. Meetings are the primary weapon of the bureaucratic forces. Meetings take place to selectively filter, package, and repackage information so that its transmission can be coordinated across departments and divisions and functions—and vertically between levels.

Venture mode obviates the need for administrative bureaucracy and its meetings by eliminating layers and instead, organizing functions as horizontal fields, not divisional silos. Administrative strata can be replaced by self-managing teams pursuing purpose-directed goals with coordinated team actions. Information is processed at the team level, and meetings can be far fewer in number and kept short.

In agile software development methodologies such as Scrum and Kanban, meetings are time-boxed to last fifteen minutes or less and are designed to synchronize efforts and address impediments, not to engage in long discussions of management issues. (They're often called "standup" meetings, because sitting down would be characteristic of an unnecessarily long meeting.) Spotify, in its "squad" model of organization around cross-functional teams, specifies fifteen-minute meetings conducted by team members standing in a circle (subject, of course, to optional innovations in meeting style by autonomous teams).

Previously siloed functions can be reframed as shared tasks with a singular purpose. For example, this concept is captured in the expression "everyone does marketing." This means that the goal of marketing—customer satisfaction—is one that everyone in the firm shares and for which they all accept responsibility. Individual marketing acts take place all over the company. These acts are unified not by a designated department called marketing but in the trusting relationship the firm's employees enjoy with customers.

Zappos, for example, famously empowers staff to deliver exceptional service and create memorable customer experience under the cultural umbrella of "delivering happiness."[11] With persistent delivery of strong, tailored value experiences, customers come to fully trust the company, or, more simply, the brand.

Venture mode avoids bureaucracy, departments, and meetings whenever possible. Actions with a low customer value score are abandoned or reduced to a minimum.

INDIVIDUALISM AND AUTONOMY

The entrepreneurial tradition of venture mode is born of individual freedom. Popular literature often portrays the entrepreneur as the brave and creative loner, fighting for market acceptance of their brilliantly innovative but not yet fully appreciated new product. There is a business role for individual creativity of course, but growth and progress result from the entrepreneurial economy as a whole, not just a few heroic geniuses.

Venture mode is the intentional pursuit of new economic value. Let's break that down.

Intentionality is the energizing long-term disposition to create value. There may be twists and turns along the way, surges of growth and periods of setbacks, learning through error correction and negative feedback. But through it all, the intention remains firm, orienting action and adaptation toward a singular purpose.

Pursuit confirms that value creation is a process: dynamic and time consuming. It requires the acceptance of uncertainty because a pursuit is not guaranteed to capture the prize. Entrepreneurship proceeds in spite of uncertainty, with mustered confidence that adaptive creativity will eventually lead to a good outcome.

New economic value refers to the improvement in customer lives through the innovation of new goods and services that customers deem useful and valuable. "New" in this case is always individual—new *to them*. So even familiar value can be entrepreneurial if it delivers new value to consumers who did not previously enjoy it. But, of course, we commonly (and rightly) ascribe a greater level of "entrepreneurialness" to innovations that are more novel to more people.

All of these are inherent to venture mode, and the mode can be adopted at any organizational level.

Yet still, the ultimate source of entrepreneurial energy is the free-minded and creatively resourceful individual. Venture mode is defined by action, and all actions are ultimately individual actions. We may speak of collectives, like companies, taking unified actions, but that is always imprecise shorthand. James Dyson, chairman of the famously innovative Dyson manufacturing company, speaks proudly of the company's hiring of individual students straight out of high school: "They don't do the obvious thing. They don't do what should be done. They start doing something else, which is much more interesting."[12]

Companies don't think or act, *people* do. Whether an individual is working in teams or units, advancing coordinated projects, or contributing to group goals by working on shared tasks, their autonomy and freedom are always critical. Individuals are the source of ideas, and individuals in collaboration improve total productivity.

GENERATIVE BUSINESS MODELS

A typical result from these venture mode principles is a systematic value creation business model designed to produce and sustain continuous innovation, growth, and value over time, often by leveraging the network effects and feedback loops inherent in the digital economy.

There are a few key aspects that venture mode highlights:

- **User-driven value creation:** Since venture mode focuses tightly on the end user and specifically on understanding their most pressing needs for well-being, entrepreneurs structure business models in such a way that users, customers, or participants contribute to generating new value. They do this by interacting with the business platform, especially to get things done. This way, users purposefully share data with the business, from which entrepreneurial deduction draws insights and recognizes patterns. Venture mode emphasizes marketplaces and ecosystems where user participation drives further engagement and accelerates and multiplies value creation.

Facebook is a good example. Users share data—i.e., post their pictures and messages—which communicates both to Facebook and to everyone else on the network what's trending and what's subjectively important. Other people comment and "like," which is more information about preferences. Facebook can identify trends and make the appropriate business decisions to enhance the joy of sharing on the platform.

- **Network effects:** Venture mode is especially attuned to the power of networks since creative entrepreneurs seek to combine and recombine assets and resources that they don't necessarily own or command. As these entrepreneurs engage more users with their expanding service network, the worth of their network increases, attracting more users and more suppliers, which leads to exponential growth.

  Generative models are often built to scale rapidly as network effects amplify their impact, as seen in platforms like Airbnb and Uber. Both were started by under-resourced entrepreneurs aiming to assemble a network of similarly under-resourced collaborators to create value together.

- **AI and automation:** Venture mode eagerly seeks ways to increase capacity without adding fixed assets, and AI and automation are a perfect fit. More and more AI tools are emerging for entrepreneurs to use and explore, resulting in new outputs, services, or innovations, and creating new kinds of value through the combination of AI and human input. AI can even identify sentiments through pattern recognition, providing empathic humans with more insights into customer motivations.

- **Open-ended innovation:** Entrepreneurial leaders love models that are not limited to a single product or service offering but are designed to enable ongoing innovation. They prefer unbounded opportunity spaces with the chance to explore without necessarily having a fixed destination in mind. They are not afraid of experimentation, comfortable in the knowledge that markets will select those experiments that meet their needs, sending feedback to the entrepreneur about where to expand their efforts and which dead-end paths to abandon.

A DIFFERENT LOGIC

Administration mode applies a logic of control, with administrators prioritizing oversight and predictability. They'd prefer to eliminate all variance from the prescribed pathway to the predicted end point. When variation is repressed in this way, creativity, innovation, and opportunity are excluded. In administration mode, change is the enemy.

Venture mode utilizes a logic of freedom. Here, customers are free to express their preferences, explore their opportunities, report on their experiences, and generally lead the way to innovation. Knowledge flows freely from markets to every location and every individual in the firm.

Creative ideas are freely expressed, with a spirit of exploration and experimentation to test, prove, and assess their readiness for implementation. Variance is not avoided but sought out as a signal of possible new learning and insight, rather than viewed as a loss of control.

In sum, venture mode is a dynamic, exciting possibility space, a roaring river of creative currents. It doesn't have a rulebook. It's not neat or tidy. It's fast and resourceful and can look messy to administrators. It's betting on what could be, not managing what already exists. Nothing is inherited, everything is created. Venture mode is creating the future, not predicting it.

CHAPTER 6

VENTURE MODE VERSUS THE BUSINESS SCHOOL

In the business school, strategy is like a game of chess that you're playing against one or more competitors. The goal is what professors call "competitive advantage." In their world of administration, firms strive for competitive differentiation—to be notably different from the competitors' alternatives, better on some dimension of quality, features, or cost.

The measure of effective strategy is persistently higher performance. As a general rule of thumb, firms must rank number one or two in a competitive market for the strategy to be deemed successful. Achieving such a rank is a militaristic battle of wits, conducted aggressively by deploying the firm's "strength" and "power" to "beat the competition."

So strategy is depicted as an indispensable requirement for successful business practice. One leading business school professor has even stated that the only bad strategy is *not* having a strategy.[1] And its centrality to academic thinking about business performance has led to strategic management becoming the capstone course that all business students must take.

Business schools, therefore, have developed a set of tools that they teach to support the development, implementation, and achievement of good strategy and consequent competitive advantage.

But this is all wrong. Business school strategy focuses on the wrong things, diverting attention and energy from what really matters for the long term: value-creating entrepreneurship.

THE BUSINESS ADMINISTRATION CURRICULUM

It was back in the 1950s that prescient business guru Peter Drucker wrote that innovation and marketing are the only two legitimate business functions. All the rest, he said, are just costs. This is still right, but it seemed like nobody at business school listened. A typical business administration curriculum will include these classes:

- **Financial Accounting:** the principles and practices of financial reporting
- **Managerial Accounting:** internal use of accounting information for decision-making
- **Corporate Finance:** concepts like capital structure, valuation, risk management, and investment decision-making
- **Economics for Managers:** an understanding of microeconomic and macroeconomic principles and market structures for managerial decision-making
- **Marketing Management:** marketing principles such as market research, consumer behavior, branding, pricing strategies, and digital marketing trends
- **Operations Management:** examination of production and service delivery, focusing on supply chain management, process optimization, and quality control

- **Organizational Behavior:** human behavior in organizations and organizational culture
- **Business Analytics:** data analysis, statistical methods, and decision-making tools
- **Ethics and Corporate Social Responsibility (CSR):** ethical decision-making, corporate governance, and the role of businesses in society
- **Strategic Management:** the capstone course—frameworks for analyzing industry dynamics, identifying competitive advantages, and making strategic business decisions

With the possible exception of marketing management, it is reasonable to classify all of these courses as sitting on the cost side of Drucker's contrasting business functions. Innovation is often featured as an elective course and is often taught as a mechanical process rather than as the creative mindset of meeting customers' subjective needs. Similarly, marketing management often focuses on tools such as market research and mechanics such as digital marketing and pricing—less so on the subjective, humanistic, empathic, and emotional customer relationship building discovered via deep understanding of end user motivations.

Of course, the crowning jewel of the curriculum for prospective business leaders is the capstone course: strategic management.

THE TRADITIONAL TOOLS OF BUSINESS STRATEGY

Business schools have taught the same traditional tools of business strategy for decades. These tools include the SWOT analysis, the VRIO framework of the resource-based view (RBV), Porter's Five Forces, and PESTEL. Each of these frameworks reflects a worldview rooted in administration—static environments, predictable competition, and linear cause-and-effect dynamics—which are poorly aligned with the realities of a digital, hyperconnected, and rapidly evolving marketplace. Here's why.

1. SWOT Analysis

The SWOT analysis (strengths, weaknesses, opportunities, threats) is a technique to analyze the strategic position of an organization or business. It's barely useful when done right, and it's almost never done right.[2]

There are two versions of the SWOT analysis that are potentially helpful. In the first, the SWOT is set up as a typology. Its quadrants are not strengths, weaknesses, opportunities, and threats, but strengths-opportunities, weaknesses-opportunities, strengths-threats, and weaknesses-threats. The goal of this approach is to discover which strengths to build and leverage to take advantage of which opportunities and, on the other hand, which weaknesses are vulnerable to real threats and need to be shored up.

In the second version, the normal SWOT is performed—the strengths, weaknesses, opportunities, and threats are listed in each quadrant—not just for the focal firm but also *for each competitor*. This then allows the strategist to ascertain which opportunities they can pursue that are not well suited to their competitors and which threats their competitors bring that the focal firm needs to guard against.

The *best* SWOT, of course, would be when both of these approaches are combined.

But what students are *actually* taught is to fill in the four boxes—strengths, weaknesses, opportunities, and threats—for the focal firm only. Thus, the firm analyzed learns essentially nothing at all. The boxes are filled with precisely what the firm already knows about itself and its industry.

But even if it was done "right," using the best version of the analysis, the SWOT is problematic. From the beginning, the analysis assumes a stable environment where a firm can assess fixed internal and external factors to devise a strategy. Moreover, there are no fixed, given opportunities out there for the analyst to determine and assess. And threats generally "come out of nowhere." If they were just sitting there, able to be ascertained by any analyst, then any strategic manager worth their salt would be aware of them and monitoring them.

But, of course, the contemporary business landscape is *actually* characterized by constant flux, where opportunities and threats are dynamic and spontaneous. What's more, the sets of opportunities available to the firm are not those seen and listed by an analyst. Such opportunities are barely worth the attention. The real opportunities are those *created* through the ingenuity of entrepreneurs.

The SWOT analysis lacks mechanisms to incorporate feedback from dynamic and emergent change within and around the industry. SWOT's static approach to mapping the business environment is no match for the fluid, real-time strategic adjustments required in a modern market.

2. The Resource-Based View

The resource-based view (RBV) is a management framework that focuses on leveraging and protecting a firm's unique strategic resources and capabilities to achieve a sustainable competitive advantage. In fact, RBV strongly implies that strategic resources are only possible to obtain by "endowment" or "luck."[3] If they can be built, they're not strategic resources because competitors can do the same.

Its most familiar implementation is in the VRIN or VRIO analytical framework.[4] This tool aids the strategist in assessing the strategic nature of its resources. The user lists the firm's various resources and then assesses them according to the VRIO decision tree.

First, is the resource *valuable*? That is, does it improve the competitive position of the firm in some way? If not, it's not a strategic resource.

But if so, is it also *rare*? That is, are they the only company in the industry with that resource? If not, the resource produces only competitive parity, allowing the firm to compete on par with competitors that also have the resource. Of course, the company can feasibly use that resource better than its competitors, but we can only expect that to be the case temporarily.

If it *is* rare, is it also *inimitable* (and non-substitutable)? That is, if it's a strategically valuable resource that other competitors don't have, can they get it? Can they copy it? Can they find a workaround that works as well? If so, the strategic advantage purveyed by the resource is only temporary.

But if not, if it *is* inimitable (if it's patented, for example), then the resource may be the source of a sustainable competitive advantage. But scholars have added a fourth criterion: Is the firm *organized* to effectively capture the value of the resource? Poor organization and execution can lead to an underexploited resource, essentially leaving much or all of its value on the table.

Recall from chapter two how Xerox employed many of the world's most talented engineers at its famous Palo Alto Research Center. It was these engineers who really designed the modern computer. The Alto computer design was completed in 1973. It had a graphical user interface, a trackball mouse, Ethernet email, laser printing, and so on. But the leadership at Xerox on the opposite coast were never persuaded of the value of this project. Computers, at the time, were widely understood to have limited applications.

In 1977, Ken Olsen, CEO of Digital Equipment Corporation, infamously claimed that "there is no reason for any individual to have a computer in his home" at a meeting of the World Future Society.[5]

But the biggest irony is that Xerox leadership gave Steve Jobs (and later his whole team) an in-depth demonstration of the computer technology on which Xerox PARC researchers had been working for years. Jobs immediately saw the opportunity in it. And, of course, he took it.

The RBV and its VRIO analysis tool can be useful as long as they're not taken too seriously, but there is a fundamental problem with it: Value is *subjective*. It's simply wrong to say that resources *have* value or that they *are* valuable, as we explained in the previous chapter. Of course, that's how people talk, and we understand what people mean when they say such things. But it's not strictly true. Resources aren't intrinsically *valuable*, they are *valued*.

What this means is that value is fundamentally subjective—it depends on what people think about it—and so it can change at a whim. And it does.

Research in Motion (or RIM, now BlackBerry) owned extremely valuable resources in its proprietary IP, brand name and reputation, and first-mover advantages in the mid-2000s. Any RBV analyst would describe RIM as having a sustainable competitive advantage due to its strong strategic resources.

A few short years later, it was forced to exit the smartphone industry altogether. Its "valuable" strategic resources were no match for the innovations introduced in Apple's iPhone. RIM's last-ditch effort to imitate Apple's technology in a 2010 product launch (the BlackBerry 10) flopped. The reification of value as a stable characteristic of RIM's strategic resources led to a false understanding of the stability of its strategic position and the propensity of that advantage to dissolve in a moment.

3. Porter's Five Forces

The Five Forces framework, famously articulated and developed by Professor Michael Porter of Harvard Business School, is designed to evaluate industry structure and determine competitive intensity, assuming a world of discrete firms competing for market share. The five forces are competitive rivalry, supplier power, buyer power, threat of substitution, and threat of new entry. To the extent that these forces are strong, they put downward pressure on the profitability of the industry, pushing margins down.

Again, this is and has been a useful analytical framework for many years. But it has always been problematic in some ways, its flaws becoming glaring in the modern, digital era.

One fundamental issue is that Porter's concept of *industry boundaries* has always been ill-defined, and these boundaries have become increasingly blurred. Ecosystems, platforms, globalization, and cross-industry collaborations in modern markets have come to redefine competition.

To take just one example, Apple is no longer just a technology company bound by the confines of the tech industry. Its ecosystem spans media, health, and finance, and it is a services company as much as it is a technology company. How would a Five Forces framework describe the structure of the "industry" for Apple?

Management scholars have, to some extent, adapted to this problematization. Clayton Christensen taught that the industry is best defined by the "job to be done,"[6] that which consumers hire a (specific) product or service to do. This means that most larger companies, like Apple, are not in a single industry, as students and analysts tend to assume, but *many* industries—its iPhone does a different job for consumers than its laptops or its entertainment streaming services.

The analyst goes astray when trying to pigeonhole a company with many products into a single industry, because identifying the relevant competitors is confounded. But when you identify the many industries it competes in, managers and analysts can readily identify the relevant competitors, who also have products that do the same job.

This solution seems intuitively satisfactory, as it addresses the problem to an extent. But it's not. If we take Christensen's logic to its ultimate conclusion, then every differentiated product is in its own unique industry because it does a different job than other products. So where do we draw the line between *what* the job is (industry) versus *how* it is done (strategy)? In the end, this is simply a subjective judgment.

But the more fundamental problem with this framework is the problem of *equifinality.* It turns out that any specific job to be done can be done *any number of ways.* There is nothing inherent to the task that mandates that it must be done this way or that. Instead, solutions are innovated by entrepreneurial firms to solve a consumer need, and industries tend to form around that technological solution until another entrepreneurial firm comes along with a new and better idea.

The problem with this industry analysis framework now becomes clear: It assumes that the industry is well defined. Worse, it impels the manager or analyst to assume that this existing solution to the job to be done is the *only one.* As a result of this static analytical tool, managers are frequently caught ill-prepared for the almost-inevitable industry disruptions that eventually come.

The old idea of a firm building strategy within an identifiable industry with defined and stable boundaries is just no longer viable. The new environment requires continuous adaptation within dynamic market landscapes. There's a whirl of uncertainty around competitors, suppliers, and buyers that can't be subjected to static analysis, and substitution and new entry are not threats but a persistent condition of the ecosystem.

4. PESTEL

The PESTEL analysis offers a high-level overview of external factors affecting a business. It is an acronym for the six external factors that can affect an industry: political, economic, sociocultural, technological, ecological, and legal. (Sometimes it is referred to as a STEEP or PEST analysis, depending on how many factors are included.) By observing the external factors around the industry, strategic managers can better predict and prepare for impending changes.

But as this analysis is typically taught and performed, analysts assume a linear, cause-and-effect relationship between these factors and strategic decisions. Yet in reality, the interplay of these factors is often nonlinear and unpredictable. For example, technological disruptions like AI are not just "external forces" but transformative catalysts reshaping internal capabilities, customer expectations, business ecosystems, and competitive landscapes.

So the PESTEL analysis generally lacks the agility to deal with the rapid pace of change and unpredictability in modern environments. It provides a snapshot, but today's firms require dynamic, continuous monitoring and adaptation. As a static diagnostic tool, PESTEL is no match for the emergent, adaptive thinking required in contemporary strategy.

THE MISMATCH BETWEEN TRADITIONAL STRATEGY TOOLS AND MODERN REALITIES

These traditional frameworks were developed during the *twentieth century*, an era defined by

- **Linearity:** Problems could be broken down into discrete components and solved through static analysis.
- **Predictability:** Market dynamics were stable enough to allow for long-term forecasting and planning.
- **Cost efficiency:** Strategy emphasized minimizing costs and maximizing efficiency, with success often tied to economies of scale.

However, the twenty-first-century strategic landscape demands tools that accommodate

- **Dynamic adaptation:** Firms must continuously evolve, responding in real time to consumer feedback, technological change, and competitive shifts.
- **Ecosystem thinking:** Growth opportunities arise from relationships, networks, partnerships, and the ability to leverage external resources, not just internal capabilities.
- **Emergent strategy:** Strategies are not the product of analytic design that shapes predetermined plans but of discovery through experimentation and iteration.
- **User-centricity:** The focus is on delivering value to individual users through hyperpersonalization, not on achieving static market share goals.

STRATEGIZING IN VENTURE MODE

An entrepreneurial leader *does* need strategy. But it isn't the strategy of the textbooks. It's fluid, adaptive, and human. Static tools for strategic positioning are focused on the wrong key player: the competition. Your competitors don't decide if you win or not. *Consumers* do. If they prefer you over your competitors, you have a winning strategy. It sounds simple, and it is. But you'd be surprised how easy it is for businesses to lose sight of consumers as they focus on their competitors.

Differentiating for Consumers

Whereas traditional business strategy evokes differentiation from competitors by mapping out competitors' strategic positions and staking a claim on a market segment where other competitors are absent, a consumer focus arrives at a strategic position vis-à-vis user empathy. In other words, it's not about being *different* from competitors. It's about being *better* for consumers.

As a silly example of product differentiation, Droga5 (a marketing agency) launched an April Fools prank commercial in which Quilted Northern launched a "rustic weave" line of "authentic, bespoke, raw, artisanally crafted toilet paper."[7] They were highlighting the silliness of the idea, but it's remarkable how close to this sort of microcultural feature and attribute differentiation strategists can get.

They're looking in the wrong direction. In truth, the new differentiators lie in the subjective quality of direct, empathy-based *relationships* with customers. As Jeff Bezos put it when he was CEO of Amazon, "We're not competitor obsessed, we're customer obsessed."[8] Strategic advantage, in venture mode, essentially means that consumers prefer you because you have a better product or service in one or more ways that are important to them.

What this means is that there is no such thing as "competitive advantage"—only a *consumer advantage.*

The modern digitization of markets makes this distinction between competitive advantage and consumer advantage clear. Today, technology, not marketing tactics, provides the primary route to consumer engagement.

The old idea of competitive advantage is built on the functionality of one firm designing, making, distributing, advertising, retailing, or maintaining some good or service better than other firms. This approach is founded on the cost-based thinking of administration mode—seeking lower marginal costs through economies of scale and lower transactional costs through increased efficiencies, cost reduction, and error correction (on which techniques like Six Sigma are based).

In the digital era, this thinking is redundant, since marginal costs for software and other intellectual property-based components are virtually zero. Moreover, global supply chains can be configured online, new technologies can be adopted and implemented as soon as they are available, and speed and low cost are the results of efficient networks.

The venture mode idea of a consumer advantage, in contrast, is built on producing a product or service that consumers prefer for whatever reason. The standard presumption that there are a set number of differentiating options that competitors can position on (e.g., low cost, higher quality) is false. The reasons consumers might prefer one product to another are numerous—indeed literally infinite—although the imaginative mind is bounded and can only conceive of but a sliver of such possibilities. But the consumer focus drives the strategist to learn from consumers what to improve and how to improve, rather than deciding based on a strategic map.

One instance of the novelty of the modern strategic landscape, exemplified by the customer-obsessed Amazon, is network effects. A network effect emerges when a product or service becomes more valuable to consumers as the number of users grows. For example, the more sellers on Amazon's platform, the more attractive it is for buyers, and *vice versa*. Network effects provide the dynamics behind many successful software businesses, including Google, Salesforce, and Facebook. NFX studied digital companies that went on to become worth more than $1 billion and estimated that network effects account for approximately 70 percent of the value creation in tech.[9]

Open Innovation

Within the traditional model of establishing a competitive advantage, innovation comes from inside the firm. Innovation is generated via investment in R&D and new product/service development by internal teams. Innovation is possibly supplemented by contracted external contributors, but nonetheless, it remains an internal function.

But in the modern strategic landscape, where more businesses are seeking a *consumer advantage*, new models of open innovation are emerging that aim to develop innovation ecosystems comprising partnerships across industry boundaries, including universities, research labs, industry associations, governments, and NGOs.

Innovation is not limited to tangible products and services; it also includes new ways of organizing and collaborating and changing worldviews and mental models. For some generative platforms, like Google and Amazon, a considerable portion of innovation is driven by consumers finding new and better ways to use the services available to them.

In venture mode, the creation of new knowledge and relationships is key to the organization's success, and the business is organized accordingly. This sets them apart from administrative organizations focused on and organized around stable assets.

Hyperpersonalization

In the past, control-focused marketing aimed to influence consumers in what they wanted. In today's markets, where consumers are digitally and directly connected to producers, consumers more directly determine what's produced and supplied than ever before. Every individual consumer can register their preferences with producers, whether by buying or abstaining, clicking, scrolling, reading, rating, commenting, posting, and connecting their digital devices to networks that immediately produce actionable data.

When Paramount released a trailer for a new Sonic the Hedgehog movie featuring a redesign of the hedgehog's appearance, consumer feedback was rapid, passionate, and negative. Director Jeff Fowler personally addressed fans on Twitter: "Thank you for the support. And the criticism. The message is loud and clear. . . . You aren't happy with the design & you want changes. It's going to happen. Everyone at Paramount & Sega are fully committed to making this character the BEST he can be."[10]

Traditional strategies of target marketing and market segmentation are simply not as useful in today's world of hyperpersonalization. It's no longer viable to think in terms of segment averages, representative users, or demographics. Each individual consumer can get exactly what they want when and where they want it at a price they're willing to pay. The quality and depth of the personalized relationships with consumers become the keys to a firm's success.

Risk Versus Uncertainty

Much of traditional strategic planning taught in business school is driven by risk aversion. Risk is viewed as a quantifiable variable utilizing probability analysis. Using mathematical tools and models, firms calculate an expected return for any investment, resource allocation, or R&D project and then qualify these expected returns with risk probabilities. Strategists then choose between alternatives based on the numbers that are generated.

Businesses in venture mode know that this supposed precision in statistical analysis is false. The world is not composed of objective statistics. Probabilities are a construction based on personal or collective judgments and (often doubtful) assumptions. Analysts group things or occurrences into similar "cases," which can then be enumerated as statistics. But what "counts" and what doesn't is hardly objective—probabilities are not hard numbers, they're *guesses*. A probability, indeed, can only rarely be said to "exist" at all. More often than not, classification into statistics *misleads* more than it illuminates.

In venture mode, businesses don't attempt to calculate risk or expected future values. An entirely different concept is used: *uncertainty*. Uncertainty is a subjective relationship with the future, an expectation of what could happen without total confidence that it will. Venture mode recognizes that the future is unpredictable. Entrepreneurial leaders are never certain about their forecast expectations. Certainty in and strategic commitment to a forecast is a recipe for disaster.

Uncertainty is the frame of mind that results from considering unpredictability. But, in venture mode, the uncertainty that paralyzes administrators who rely on predictive analytics is transformed into a powerful strength. Venture mode entrepreneurs bypass unpredictability, taking a different tack to their destination—they *envision* a possible future and then navigate their way toward it through experimenting, testing, and feedback adjustments.

Reid Hastie eloquently differentiated administration mode's probabilistic reasoning from venture mode's uncertainty reasoning with an analogy to seafaring:

> The image of a decision maker standing at a choice point like a fork in a road and choosing one direction or the other is probably much less appropriate for major everyday decisions than the image of a boat navigating a rough sea with a sequence of many embedded choices and decisions to maintain a meandering course toward the ultimate goal.[11]

In venture mode, judgment isn't statistical but experimental. Venture mode companies don't assess options probabilistically—they *test* them. Does this option navigate us closer to our goal? A *yes* paves the way for another step in that direction. A *no* prompts learning and a pivot to another step, a turn of the captain's wheel. No statistics, no probabilities, just learning and discovery. Unpredictable? Of course. But navigable.

Systems Thinking

Business strategy's emphasis on optimization, efficiency, and planning is rooted in a linear cause-and-effect mentality. If a business takes the strategically best actions, good results will follow. Often, this cause-and-effect relationship is deduced retrospectively: Y was the outcome; therefore X must be the cause. This approach assumes that specific measurements can be isolated and targeted for improvement without accounting for intricately interconnected system interactions.

Modern digital businesses have escaped the limits of this linear thinking by developing and harnessing *systems thinking*. Systems thinkers embrace the complexity of the interconnected systems in which they operate. The study of complex systems is relatively new and still evolving, but it already offers significant advances in how systems work.

One of the core concepts of complex systems is *emergence*. Emergence is the process of new patterns of order forming unpredictably out of the interactions of individuals and components, and these new patterns exert influence on the system as a whole. Think of social media platforms, such as TikTok. The interactions of individuals have created new patterns of influence that change behavior in conversation, purchasing, and socializing. The key point about emergence is that it can't be managed. Management implies control and prediction. Emergence can't be controlled, and its outcomes can't be predicted. But they *can* be explored through entrepreneurial experimentation.

The science tells us that all systems are continuously evolving and always changing—otherwise they die. As they evolve, systems are capable of autonomously exploring and producing many different combinations and configurations of their individual components and parts.

In Darwinian fashion, the most functional configurations are selected by end users. But these configurations, and which are selected, are dynamic (continually changing) or even novel (new to the world).[12] The selection criteria are called *acceptance functions*,[13] which direct the system into areas of higher value.

In business systems, the acceptance function resides with consumers in their perceptions of value. The exploration of alternative value propositions is the entrepreneurial function.

For example, Airbnb tests different value propositions in its listings by creating two versions, each with one element changed, then showing each version to a target audience. They identify which version performed better by the number of bookings, thereby improving their listings over time. Airbnb tests one variable at a time, iterating the tests so that multiple variables in multiple combinations are evaluated by customers. By iterating A/B tests, Airbnb's value propositions are continuously refined.

Systems thinking directs entrepreneurial leaders to consider business systems as a whole, to explore different configurations, instead of trying to isolate singular causes and effects. It pushes entrepreneurial leaders to discover consumers' acceptance criteria through experimentation, to respond to results without bias, and to proceed as so directed. This is venture mode in a nutshell.

Networks of Competence

Traditional organizational thinking has produced multilayered hierarchies of managerial authority and siloed structures with specialized functions as the standard for organizing business firms. But the new science of systems lays groundwork for viewing organizations as networks rather than hierarchies, emphasizing interconnectedness and interdependence. Peter Drucker's management theories highlighting the role of knowledge workers and decentralized decision-making were part of this shift. Instead of chains of authority, the knowledge economy privileges competence and leverages it across organizational boundaries. Japanese innovations such *kaizen*[14] emphasize cross-functional collaboration and networked competence.

The rise of digital technologies and agile frameworks has expanded the practical application of networks of competence, with the ability to fluidly assemble, then disband teams as needed. Flexibility, trust, and autonomy replace top-down authority as the characteristics of decentralized networks. They expand beyond firm boundaries, building ecosystems of innovation and collaboration that extend to complementary business partnerships, supplier firms, research specialists, universities, government grants, and nonprofits.

Success gravitates to network combinations capable of systematically orchestrating the highest functionality and facilitating the most value for consumers. Think of the modern bundles of streaming video content: Disney subscribers can stream Hulu titles and some HBO content on the Disney+ platform; Hulu subscribers can access most Max content on the Hulu app; and there's only one bill.

IS ADMINISTRATION MODE EVER JUSTIFIABLE?

While much of the contemporary business landscape demands agility, adaptability, and innovation, is it possible that there are cases where remaining in administration mode, with its structured processes, hierarchical control, and emphasis on predictability, may still be justifiable?

Such instances seem to occur in environments characterized by stability, or the clearly defined boundaries that Professor Michael Porter wrote about, or perhaps where external constraints favor continuity over change.

1. Stable and Bounded Industries

In industries with long-established boundaries, well-defined value chains, and limited technological disruption, traditional managerial approaches may still hold relevance. For example,

- **Utilities:** Power companies and water providers often operate in tightly regulated, stable markets with little variability in customer demand or competitive dynamics.
- **Heavy manufacturing:** Some sectors, like large-scale industrial equipment manufacturing, may experience slower cycles of change, where efficiency and consistency are

paramount. In such cases, the focus on process optimization, cost control, and predictable output aligns well with managerial approaches rooted in stability and control.

2. Regulatory Compliance and Risk Management

In highly regulated industries, such as healthcare, finance, or aviation, the need to comply with federal or international regulations can severely constrain experimentation and agility. For example,

- **Banks:** Banks and other financial services firms must adhere to strict capital requirements and risk management protocols.
- **Pharmaceutical firms:** These organizations must meet rigorous testing and approval standards for new drugs.

Here, the penalties for deviation are so significant that adhering to administrative norms may not only be prudent but essential. Predictability and accountability are nonnegotiable, and the cost of noncompliance outweighs the potential benefits of innovation.

3. Operational Necessity in Specific Firms

Some businesses, by their very nature, may find that their existing methods are the only viable way to operate. For instance,

- **Critical infrastructure:** Industries like air traffic control or telecom networks are essential to national functioning and public safety, requiring maximum reliability and minimal deviation from established procedures.
- **High-risk environments:** These settings, including chemical and nuclear power plants, require highly rigid

processes to ensure safety and reliability, justifying the use of strict protocols and limited autonomy.

In these cases, the risks of failure—whether operational, reputational, or human—can justify sticking to traditional approaches.

But Is Administration Mode Ever Truly Effective?

These examples seem to suggest that administration mode may be strategically useful or even unavoidable. Perhaps. We think not. More likely, its persistence reflects an inability to imagine alternative approaches—which is the essence of venture mode—rather than genuine necessity. Even in the cases outlined above, a closer examination reveals cracks in the argument for administrative rigidity:

- **Stable industries are rarely truly stable.** Even utilities and heavy manufacturing are being reshaped by digitization, renewable energy, technological innovation, and new consumer demands, as well as globalization of competition and the M&A activities of foreign firms. Stability is always a temporary illusion, whatever the industry, and clinging to it is very likely to hinder long-term survival.
- **Regulatory compliance doesn't preclude innovation.** While compliance imposes constraints, it need not dictate how a firm organizes or innovates. Fintech companies have shown how highly regulated industries can still be agile and consumer focused while adhering to regulations. New thinking in compact nuclear power generation for AI data centers demonstrates how new demands can bring new solutions to market despite regulatory constraints.

- **Operational necessity can be reimagined.** Even in critical infrastructure, systems thinking and adaptive approaches can improve outcomes without compromising safety. For example, air traffic control is exploring more decentralized, AI-driven models that enhance efficiency and resilience.

THE RISKS OF STAYING IN ADMINISTRATION MODE

The ultimate danger of staying in administration mode is the inherent fragility it engenders. Businesses that rely on rigid structures and predictable routines risk being blindsided by shifts they can't see coming. By contrast, even in stable or regulated industries, firms that embrace venture mode—incorporating dynamic thinking, decentralized decision-making, and continuous learning—are better positioned to adapt to unexpected changes.

Rather than framing administration mode as a necessary fallback, firms should strive for a hybrid approach that combines operational discipline where needed with the flexibility and creativity demanded by a rapidly evolving world. In most cases, staying in administration mode reflects a failure to embrace the tools and mindsets of the future rather than a genuine requirement of the business environment.

In the end, depending on traditional knowledge and analysis, traditional experiences, traditional methods, and traditional skills will prove unable to cope with the challenges of complexity and rapid technological and human change. A new way of thinking is called for.

When companies like Tesla, SpaceX, Amazon Web Services, Nvidia, and Uber Eats grow explosively into spaces that didn't exist a short time ago, it's a signal that new ways of entrepreneurial thinking, new value frameworks, new organizational principles, and new management methods and tools are needed.

CHAPTER 7

HOW TECHNOLOGY ENABLES VENTURE MODE

The steam engine spawned new industries, businesses, and user experiences in a cultural, social, and market phenomenon we now call the Industrial Age. Steam power became near-ubiquitous in industrially developed countries as a great enhancer of well-being. Entrepreneurs both catalyzed the evolution of technological advances and saw opportunities these new technologies promised for better consumer experiences.

Thomas Savery patented his early steam engine in 1698 for commercial purposes, seeing applications in supplying water to estates and country houses and for raising water from mines, which was an important "job to be done" for the mining industry of his time. Thomas Newcomen further developed Savery's design into a much more effective prototype, better at pumping water out of flooded mines.

The James Watt steam engine of 1776 was a further technological advance—adding a separate condenser—that became the pivotal advance for broadscale use in factories and railroads, enabling both mass production and mass transportation. It was a tipping point innovation. Watt's technological breakthroughs unleashed a tidal wave of factories, railways, and urban growth no one could have foreseen.

Kerosene distillation was a quirky chemical trick that John D. Rockefeller turned into a nationwide lighting revolution, fueling productivity and comfort in homes far beyond chemists' imagination. Today, AI is being forged by entrepreneurs to wrestle with knowledge itself, lighting the fuse to the next industrial age.

In venture mode, technological progress becomes an exciting enabler. Venturers are animated by the adaptive fluidity, the potential for innovation, and the new possibilities that exist within technological uncertainty. Organizations operating in venture mode align themselves with technology's natural flow, both leading and leveraging.

This mindset contrasts sharply with traditional business administration, which finds technology to be a constant threat—it's one of those PESTEL external factors to be wary of. Consequently, administrators often seek to impose preconceived processes and frameworks to govern technological adoption. In the more radical (but unfortunately not uncommon) cases, they lobby governments to prohibit technologies or, at least, render them prohibitively costly. Where this occurs, entrepreneurship in that market is halted and the market stalls.

In this chapter, we review modern technological progress from the vantage of venture mode. In this abbreviated history, we can see the synergy of autonomous technological advancement and adaptive entrepreneurial action all around us in the systems we use every day. It's hard to look at what entrepreneurs have built for us without a profound sense of gratitude—even awe—for the great comforts and pleasures we now enjoy.

After this historical overview, we'll turn our attention toward understanding the synergies between technology and venture mode. Businesses in venture mode are inherently technological, and one of the great benefits of technology is the incremental displacement of administration with technology. But we note that the essence of venture mode, the entrepreneurial mindset, can never be replaced by technology.

TECHNOLOGY'S PROGRESS IN VENTURE MODE

The Internet as a Catalyst for Entrepreneurial Disruption

Let's start with the advent of hyperconnectivity through internet technology. The first form of internet was originally developed as a government research project (ARPANET), connecting computers for the sharing of research data. Today, entrepreneurs have evolved the internet into a ubiquitous platform that has proven to be transformative for industries like retail, media, and communication. Indeed, almost no business in the modern economy could operate without the internet, and those businesses (in administration mode) who were slow to develop an online presence were punished, sometimes fatally.

Infrastructure giants like Amazon and Alibaba established internet-based e-commerce technology platforms, and both they and the independent sellers who operate on the platforms leveraged the internet to pioneer new business models that replaced traditional retail hierarchies with decentralized networks, substituting direct home delivery for brick-and-mortar shopping. Entrepreneurial sellers built multimillion-dollar businesses on the infrastructure that Alibaba and Amazon made available to them. This was in no way a vision or a purpose of the original US Department of Defense project and could not have happened without entrepreneurial imagination.

Artificial Intelligence and Machine Learning

AI originated as a niche academic and scientific research discipline with limited commercial applications. Its breakthrough moments, such as deep learning algorithms, were the result of cumulative advancements in computational power and data availability.

Entrepreneurs now put AI to use in major business transformations, such as predictive analytics in finance, personalized recommendations in streaming platforms, autonomous vehicles in logistics, and AI agents to automate numerous tasks and govern digitally monitored processes, freeing up human time for creativity and imagination. Aggregators like There's An AI For That (TAAFT)[1] make tens of thousands of AI tools available for more entrepreneurs to build new businesses and customer services.

Blockchain and Decentralization

Blockchain technology, initially developed as the underlying infrastructure for Bitcoin, has evolved into a versatile tool for decentralizing trust and enabling smart contracts.

Industries such as supply chain management, healthcare, and real estate are exploring blockchain applications to eliminate intermediaries, increase transparency, and better secure contracts. In financial services, banks like UBS are developing projects for the application of blockchain technology in speeding up back-office settlement operations, and an entire new decentralized financial services industry (dubbed "fintech") has emerged as a result of entrepreneurial experimentation with blockchain technology.

Mobile Technology and App Ecosystems

Although the iPhone was a distinctive product of Apple, the rise and expansion of smartphones to their current day ubiquity was not orchestrated by a single corporate vision but emerged from the convergence of business-led advancements in wireless technology, miniaturization, and computing power.

Similarly, the explosion of mobile apps was driven by independent designers rather than the centralized corporation. While originally developing the iPhone, Apple's then-CEO Steve Jobs did not intend to let third-party developers build native apps for iOS. However, backlash from developers prompted the company to reconsider, with Apple belatedly announcing in October 2007 that there would be a software development kit available for developers by February 2008.

The ecosystem of mobile apps, now so central to the way we conduct our lives and operate our businesses, is an emergent result of the creative competition of entrepreneurial developers and programmers. They use their imagination and ingenuity to devise new services that survive or fail based entirely on end user acceptance criteria. Entire industries, such as ride-sharing (Uber, Lyft) and mobile payments (Venmo, Alipay), were born out of this mobile revolution.

Renewable Energy and Grid Decentralization

Regional utilities are one of the last bastions of the old-fashioned, large-scale production monopolies. Technologies like solar panels and battery storage evolved independently of the centralized utilities, driven by a mix of competition-driven progress and consumer demand for sustainable alternatives.

From new electricity generation technologies, combined with unlimited entrepreneurial imagination, a new industry of decentralized energy systems is emerging. Solar power generation for individual homes and commercial buildings is now a reality. New integrated systems such as electric cars and their charging grids and new battery innovations like Tesla's Powerwall are reshaping the energy industry. Centralized utilities didn't initiate the revolution—if anything they delayed it.

Rather than trying to act as master planners who direct the course of technological adoption, businesses in venture mode adopt a mindset of technological alignment. This means understanding the trajectory of emerging technologies, being attuned to their natural evolution, and identifying how these developments can unlock opportunities within the economy. Venture mode anticipates, prompts, interprets, leverages, and further advances the evolution of technology.

ENGAGING TECHNOLOGY IN VENTURE MODE

How do businesses in venture mode engage with technology? It's the fuel that drives them. It's their passion, their highest goal. Profit is but a necessary stepping stone to the ideal of a better world created by these technologists.

Listening to Technology's Signals

Instead of imposing rigid planning and development frameworks, as businesses in administration mode do, businesses in venture mode stay constantly curious and observant, asking,

- What patterns are emerging?
- How are new technologies reshaping industries, or how might they do so in the future?
- What opportunities might arise from unexpected technological developments?
- What new combinations are possible now that weren't before the new technology emerged?
- What new possibility spaces are opening up adjacent to the new technology?
- What do customers and consumers think about how technology might improve their businesses and their lives?
- What are consumers dissatisfied with today that future technology might be able to make better?

Businesses in venture mode don't necessarily feel the need to internally originate (i.e., invent) new technologies. They know that the first to invent is not necessarily the first to succeed in the marketplace. Instead, they seek to apply externally developed technologies in new ways to please consumers and open up new market revenues. Being first with a new technology is not as important as producing the best value experience for consumers.

Partnering with Technology

The entrepreneurial mindset shifts from taming and controlling technology to riding it, partnering with it as it evolves. Entrepreneurial leaders recognize that technology is not just a tool but an evolving system that offers emergent possibilities beyond immediate utility. They seek to harness its potential as it unfolds, rather than resisting its trajectory. Adopting this entrepreneurial mindset involves several key practices:

- **Nurturing a culture of experimentation:** Organizations that embrace venture mode foster experimentation, giving teams the freedom to test new technologies and learn fast about their potential. Discovery—finding out what *can* happen by running lots of experiments—is the goal, rather than planned predictability. Breakthroughs can emerge organically from exploration, and new commercial opportunities open up.
- **Identifying acceptance criteria:** Entrepreneurs quickly identify what consumers' acceptance criteria are in the marketplace. It's these acceptance criteria that determine adoption, not the technological features themselves. Waymo driverless cars have reached high adoption levels in cities like San Francisco now that they've established a safety record over fifty million driverless miles. Proving themselves against the acceptance criterion of safety,

Waymo cars enabled consumer adoption. So much so, that in 2025 the service is used for more than 250,000 paid rides per week in four US cities (Phoenix, San Francisco, Los Angeles, and Austin).[2] More cities will soon follow.

- **Leveraging uncertainty:** Instead of fearing the unpredictability of technological evolution, venture mode thrives on it. Entrepreneurs understand that uncertainty often signals the presence of new opportunities waiting to be uncovered. Instead of allowing uncertainty to deter action, entrepreneurial leaders act experimentally and then assess the opportunities that action uncovers.

Examples of a Technological Alignment Mindset in Venture Mode

In the creative world of venture mode, entrepreneurs find new adjacencies where emerging technologies can be quickly applied to create new customer value. New technology, which may yet be uncommercialized (or commercialized in one or few industries) can be quickly transformed into novel solutions by entrepreneurs, who may combine it with existing tech as a booster, integrate it into distribution systems to make it more widely relevant, or apply it in the design of new customer experiences that the technology originators never imagined. Here are some notable examples:

- **Amazon Web Services (AWS):** Amazon adopted cloud infrastructure as an efficiency tool for its own business operations. It was the customer-facing parts of Amazon that recognized the potential of the new internal cloud infrastructure as a product for external users. Rather than adhering to a preconceived strategy, Amazon aligned with (and, for a while, got ahead of) the natural evolution of cloud technology, creating a new revenue stream that the firm had never predicted and yet is now the very core of its business model.

- **Spotify's algorithmic personalization:** Spotify capitalized on the user data patterns from machine learning algorithms to introduce Discover Weekly, a curation feature that became a big hit with users, significantly increasing engagement. By aligning with AI's capabilities, Spotify enhanced the user experience and differentiated itself in a crowded market. The machine learning was algorithmic, while the Discover Weekly feature was creative, based on deep consumer empathy. It was a feature that an algorithm could not design; it required human ingenuity. Then the algorithm was given the reins to implement.
- **Tesla's battery strategy:** Tesla identifies many adjacencies in the EV ecosystem and battery/storage technology. The decision to offer advanced battery technology for homes demonstrates the essential combinatorial thinking in venture mode—aligning breakthroughs in energy storage with a meaningfully empathic diagnosis of homeowners' diminishing confidence in the grid and their demand for sustainable alternatives.

AUTOMATING ADMINISTRATION: THE TECHNOLOGY PATHWAY TO VENTURE MODE

In opposition to the entrepreneurial agility we're describing stands the great gremlin of bureaucracy at the heart of business administration.

In a company in administration mode, bureaucracy is a feature, not a bug. There must be a hierarchy for the passing down of instructions and ensuring that they are followed. There must be processes to follow so that those higher in the hierarchy can know what the lower levels are doing and how they're doing it. There must be guardrails, boundaries, and restrictions in order to limit unexpected outcomes. There must be centralized resource allocation so as to limit independent overstepping.

This administration mode is thus characterized by rigid hierarchies, multilayered approval processes, and a heavy reliance on human intermediaries to ensure compliance, consistency, and accountability. While these structures are designed for operational control, they stifle creativity, slow innovation, and make agile adaptation nearly impossible. These qualities are antithetical to venture mode.

Most significantly, bureaucratic activities don't have the purpose of facilitating consumer value. They make procedure more important than outcomes in their aim at internal control.

Venture mode aims to obviate bureaucracy. Think of a quintessential entrepreneurial start-up in growth mode. The venture focuses 100 percent of its scarce resources on consumer value—toward understanding the consumers' needs, tailoring all development activities toward improving the value proposition, initiating and nurturing customer relationships, and responding to customer feedback.

There's an acute consciousness of the speed of decision-making since a rapid response is valued by customers. Actions that ensure survival and success are prioritized without distraction or diversion toward less vital activities. No resources can be given to functions that are not consumer facing or don't directly facilitate consumer value. Those would be viewed as waste. If a task doesn't directly facilitate consumer value, it's not absolutely necessary.

Of course, the start-up must have an accounting function to keep track of resources and cash flow, but it probably doesn't have a fully-fledged financial department generating routine reports and budgets. It will have a legal function for contracting, since contracts are fundamental to customer relationships, but no legal department for internal policing. It has DevOps to ensure customer functionality but no process bureaucracy. It will develop expertise in recruiting, since the best talent will serve customers in the best way, but it won't have the kind of HR department that publishes compliance rules and regulates employee behavior. There's no procurement department, just the function of purchasing inputs that the team agrees are necessary. There need be no centralized functions at all, since they can be delegated to frontline teams or outsourced. Nothing distracts from the two critical functions of consumer marketing and innovation.

The question the venture mode firm asks in every case is whether or not the activity directly serves customers and adds to their value experience. Customers will not be well served by a company that doesn't have the appropriate contracting skills or service capability. But there's no consumer value in resources devoted to an HR department for the purposes of internal dispute resolution. Tesla operates with minimal planning, budgeting, and HR bureaucracy, suggesting that, in venture mode, the problem of bureaucracy is not insoluble, even at large scale.

An interesting new alternative with transformative potential is now emerging: AI-powered automation. By automating repetitive tasks, streamlining processes, and enabling real-time decision-making, AI can dismantle bureaucratic bottlenecks, liberating firms to operate with the agility, creativity, and innovation that venture mode demands. It can eliminate those aspects of bureaucracy that are wasteful or diversionary in regard to customer value.

Let's step through some of the key ways technology—specifically AI—will enable the abandonment of administration mode in those companies willing to embrace the revolution.

Elimination of Bureaucratic Layers

One of the most harmful characteristics of bureaucracy is the addition of management layers, creating what is typically referred to as middle management. These layers come into being to supervise the proper implementation—i.e., did the task get done, and was it done right—of what are often routine tasks. AI systems excel at performing such tasks with speed, precision, and complete reliability, eliminating the need for human intermediaries who traditionally administer these processes.

- **Impact:** Tasks like data entry, report generation, and compliance checks can be automated, reducing the layers of bureaucracy and empowering teams to focus on value-adding activities.
- **Example:** AI-driven workflow tools like UiPath and Blue Prism automate back-office operations, reducing approval timelines and freeing up human bandwidth for strategic initiatives.

Streamlining Process Steps

Process mapping has been a typically bureaucratic activity, allocating time and effort to mapping every input and output within a defined process, creating milestones and gates to navigate between each step, and dictating how many people should be working on each step for how many hours. As a result, bureaucratized processes often involve unnecessary redundancies that slow operations. AI can map out and optimize these workflows, identifying inefficiencies and suggesting streamlined alternatives.

- **Impact:** Simplified processes improve speed to market and responsiveness to changing customer demands.
- **Example:** In supply chain management, AI tools analyze procurement, inventory, and logistics data to eliminate redundant steps and enhance efficiency.

Enhanced Decision-Making Through Real-Time Insights

Reports are one of the major products of bureaucracy. Too often, these reports are static, backward-looking, and too far removed in time from the current state to be useful in informing decisions. AI replaces reports with dynamic, real-time data and insights that enable rapid, informed decision-making.

- **Impact:** Firms can pivot quickly in response to market signals, fostering adaptability and innovation.
- **Example:** AI platforms like Salesforce Einstein provide real-time customer insights, enabling teams to respond promptly to emerging trends or issues.

Democratization of Innovation

The major point of bureaucracy is to centralize decision-making power. While this can enable organizational cohesion to a unified vision, it also creates bottlenecks and slows down innovation and overall responsiveness, as innovation teams wait for permission to proceed or for funding for their next stage of exploration. Venture mode is decentralized and permissionless, offering freedom and autonomy to frontline employees to act quickly. While this can result in disparate efforts, such an approach seems far more prudent than putting all the firm's chips on one number. Technologies, such as AI tools, can democratize access to information and decision-making capabilities, empowering teams across the organization to act autonomously in a more cohesive manner without snuffing out innovative ideation at all levels of the organization.

- **Impact:** Decentralized teams can experiment, innovate, and execute without waiting for top-down directives.
- **Example:** Tools like Google's AutoML enable employees with minimal technical expertise to develop machine learning models, fostering grassroots innovation.

Scalability Without Bureaucratic Bloating

As firms scale, traditional administrative leaders will add layers of management to handle the increased complexity. AI enables organizations to scale without proportionately increasing their bureaucratic footprint. AI can supplement and strengthen individual efforts, boost productivity, and enable them to deal with more complexity without adding control layers.

- **Impact:** Automation allows firms to manage complexity while maintaining the flat, agile structures characteristic of venture mode.
- **Example:** AI-powered customer service bots like Intercom handle millions of inquiries simultaneously, scaling customer support without requiring additional headcount.

Cultural Shift Toward the Entrepreneurial Mindset

The most important consequence of AI's ability to automate routine tasks is to encourage a cultural shift from compliance and rule following to creativity and problem-solving. When new opportunities emerge or new market changes are detected, the entrepreneurial culture is to act. That might mean taking on new work, deploying additional budget, or recruiting new team members. With the confidence that AI can automate many or all of the bureaucratic elements of change, individual employees will be freed to enter action mode without reservation.

- **Impact:** Employees can focus on ideation, strategy, and collaboration, aligning with venture mode's emphasis on innovation and adaptability.
- **Example:** Companies like Spotify automate much of their administrative workload, allowing teams to focus on developing and iterating creative projects.

AI Automation Improves Implementation

When bureaucracy falls into entrepreneurial hands, unexpectedly great developments become possible:

- **More simplicity:** Bureaucratic processes tend to become more complicated over time—more process steps, more sign-offs for approval, more regulations with which to comply. Process automation using AI can achieve the opposite—not merely digitizing existing workflows but eliminating unnecessary complexity. For example, many of the middle management positions designed for monitoring and supervision in bureaucratic systems can be eliminated when a fully operational AI automation takes over.

- **Augmented employees:** Bureaucracy can often be a limitation on human creativity, whether through job descriptions limiting how expertise can be applied or budget permissions limiting the number of trial experiments that can be run. We are just beginning to understand how to use AI in the opposite way, as a tool to augment human creativity and decision-making. Individual employees can feel more energized and resourceful knowing that AI is providing a basket of new tools to draw on. People can find knowledge they need, and they can test their own logic with AI help. AI can even help them think through the possible consequences of actions. Augmented employees can make connections between data points and variables, polish communications in ways that weren't obvious to the human analyst, improve visual representations, and write new code or improve existing code. What future employees will be able to do in creating new value is exciting.
- **Iteration:** AI systems should evolve alongside the organization, ensuring that processes remain flexible and aligned with market needs. Many faults or enhancements can emerge as a result of implementing actions or processes repeatedly, faster, for longer, or with less deterioration. (AIs don't get bored!) Improvement comes faster.
- **Intensified customer-centric focus:** The ultimate judge of any business product, service, or process is the consumer. They evaluate their experience and provide feedback (often silently, e.g., by not repurchasing). AI

> automation can be tuned to refine the customer experience (making it more convenient, faster, and more accurate) and can take in feedback data of various forms (from ratings to returns) in order to further refine experience delivery. Automation, therefore, will ultimately enhance customer experience, whether by reducing response times, personalizing interactions, or improving product quality. All of these are entrepreneurial goals.

By leveraging AI to automate processes, firms can avoid the pitfalls of bureaucracy as they scale, ensuring they remain innovative and responsive. This aligns perfectly with venture mode's values of fluidity and adaptability, positioning firms for sustainable success in dynamic markets.

WHAT CAN'T BE AUTOMATED

The ultimate purpose and singular focus of venture mode is value. As we've explained, value is perceived by the customer, an understanding or recognition that they have shifted, or might shift, from a state of lower well-being to one of higher well-being. This sense of increased well-being is not mathematically calculable and can't be artificially diagnosed. Entrepreneurship aims to facilitate this sentiment, but it doesn't try to do so mechanically or artificially.

While AI is a powerful enabler of efficiency, scalability, and innovation, in many domains value is one critical element of entrepreneurship that remains fundamentally human. At its core, value involves understanding and fulfilling human needs, desires, and aspirations in a way that resonates emotionally and deeply with consumers. This process requires empathy, imagination, and the ability to envision a future that goes beyond data-driven patterns—qualities that are inherently human and resistant to automation.

1. Empathy with Consumers

- **Human understanding:** Empathy is the ability to understand the feelings of others. We can't feel what others feel, but, through empathy, we can simulate that feeling closely. Entrepreneurs connect with consumers at an emotional level, grasping the unarticulated frustrations, dreams, and aspirations that shape their behavior yet are unavailable to AI.
- **Why AI falls short:** Large language models (LLMs) like ChatGPT can analyze existing data and mimic human interaction, but they lack the lived experience and emotional intuition needed to genuinely "feel" or understand human emotions. They can only reflect patterns found in their training data; they can't generate original insights based on deep empathy.
- **Example:** Steve Jobs famously emphasized designing products that consumers didn't even know they needed—like the iPhone. Such visionary leaps require empathy-driven insights that AI cannot replicate.

2. Envisioning a Future

- **Human imagination:** Value innovation involves imagining a future that doesn't yet exist, including the mental state of a customer engaging with products, services, or experiences that defy current conventions and have no precedent in existing data. This imagination is counterfactual. It requires replacing the present with an imagined possible future based on new actions and inputs. It doesn't represent reality; it crafts a vision for a future that inspires and excites.

- **Why AI falls short:** AI models generate outputs based on patterns and probabilities within their training data, making them inherently retrospective. They excel at optimization but struggle with pure invention.
- **Example:** The creation of Airbnb involved reimagining travel and hospitality in a way that hadn't been attempted before. AI couldn't have predicted or conceptualized this model because it relied on a fundamentally new way of thinking.

3. Emotional Attachment to the Problem

- **Human passion:** In addition to imagining the future, venture mode is fueled by a fervent belief that the new future can be realized through creative effort and intense commitment. Entrepreneurs are often driven by a deep emotional connection to the problem they are solving, whether it's born from personal experience, a sense of purpose, or a desire to make the world better. This passion fuels persistence, creativity, and resilience in the face of challenges.
- **Why AI falls short:** AI lacks intrinsic motivation, emotional attachment, or a sense of purpose. It can't experience the kind of personal stakes that drive human entrepreneurs to pursue bold and risky ideas.

- **Example:** The founders of Warby Parker created their company out of frustration with the high cost of eyewear, using their personal experiences to drive a mission of affordability and style.

HUMAN VALUE IN VENTURE MODE

Venture mode elevates value as a cornerstone of its philosophy. Unlike administration mode, which often emphasizes optimization of existing processes, venture mode thrives on identifying and addressing unmet needs in ways that redefine markets. The radical consumer-centric focus of entrepreneurial leaders is bolstered by a strong empathic connection with consumers, charismatic storytelling, and the careful crafting of powerful value experiences.

1. The Role of Empathy in Innovation

Entrepreneurial firms prioritize getting close to their customers, often using tools like

- ethnographic research to observe consumers in real-life settings
- design-thinking workshops to uncover latent needs
- direct engagement through community-building and feedback loops

2. The Power of Storytelling

Entrepreneurs use storytelling to imagine and communicate a compelling vision of the future. This narrative skill inspires customers, investors, and employees to believe in a reality that doesn't yet exist.

3. The Art of Crafting Meaningful Experiences

Value in venture mode focuses not just on products or services but on the experiences that entrepreneurship makes possible. This requires deep cultural and emotional understanding that only humans can achieve.

AI AS A VALUE INNOVATION PARTNER

While AI cannot create value independently, it can play a huge supporting role in the process:

- **Amplifying insights:** AI can analyze consumer data to surface trends and patterns that entrepreneurs can then interpret and act upon.
- **Streamlining prototyping:** AI tools can accelerate the design and testing of new ideas, freeing human innovators to focus on big-picture creativity.
- **Enhancing personalization:** AI can help deliver highly personalized experiences at scale, aligning with human-designed visions of customer value.

AI will incrementally continue to take over the mindless grunt work of administration, allowing us to focus our efforts on those tasks that are uniquely human. In this sense, it'll allow us to become even more human.

A NEW THRESHOLD

In venture mode, humans remain at the center of value creation. Empathy, imagination, and emotional attachment to problems are qualities that cannot be reduced to algorithms. AI now serves as a powerful tool to amplify human potential and will continue to improve in this capacity. But it can't replace the uniquely human ability to deeply understand consumers and thereby envision and create a future that inspires and delights. AI can't perform the entrepreneurial function, not really. It can only mimic and imitate ideas that have already been developed.

Happily, we stand at the threshold of a golden age for new value creation:

- Technology is advancing autonomously at an accelerated pace, enabling, facilitating, and inspiring the value imaginations of motivated and creative entrepreneurial thinkers.
- Bureaucracy, the enemy of value innovation, is about to be tamed by automation and may be removed as a barrier to progress.
- Entrepreneurial imagination is unleashed by both the advance of technology and the demise of bureaucracy and will be augmented by AI.

Administration mode leads to a gray age. While automation might be pursued for efficiency, creativity in administration mode, counterfactual imagination, illogical belief, and unbridled passion for the impossible are strictly forbidden. If it's not predictable, administration mode doesn't want you to do it.

Administration mode can constrain but it can't unleash. Administrators may wax the skis, but they will keep you from jumping off the precipice to achieve maximum speed. They avoid risk rather than charge forward despite uncertainty. Administration mode is about making the numbers rather than changing the world. It represents the anti-entrepreneurial mindset.

We urge an active campaign to bury administration mode and the business education that promotes it.

PART III

THE FUTURE

CHAPTER 8

THE NEED FOR REFORM

To this point we've laid the problem bare—there's a massive shortage of entrepreneurial leaders in the world. The business world has been taught instead how to be good administrators. Tomes of business leadership advice focus on how to get people to do what is wanted. They teach leadership styles, such as transactional versus transformational or charismatic leadership. The bulk of leadership scholarship focuses on inspiring others, enrolling them into the vision and culture of the organization, so that they commit to it and give their all. But it's all focused on improving effort and thereby maximizing efficiency.

But the goal of top leadership shouldn't be obeisance and maximum output. That's administration mode leadership. Executive leaders are effective not because they're charismatic or convincing (or conniving) but because they're *right*. People follow leaders who say and do what they think is right.

Of course, what is "right" is subjective. But the point is that people are inspired by and will follow *entrepreneurial* leaders. Not because they're "transformational" or charismatic but because they're entrepreneurial—because they have a compelling vision for the future that excites and inspires others, and they're sure they can pull it off.

Steve Jobs is often referred to as charismatic, but that's a poor characterization. Steve was notoriously hard to work with. He was stubborn. He was hard on his people. But he had an entrepreneurial vision that compelled people to follow him. It wasn't *charisma* but entrepreneurial leadership that inspired Apple devotees. Former Apple scientist Larry Tessler recounted of Jobs's leadership, "He wanted *you* to be great. And he wanted you to create something that was great. And he was going to *make* you do that."[1]

Elon Musk is another such example. Interpersonal skills are *not* Elon's forte. He's self-identified as being on the spectrum.[2] He struggles to empathize. It is hard to call him "charismatic" in any real or meaningful sense. Like Jobs, he's hard on his employees. He often runs them through essentially manufactured crises (they're real problems, but not the crises he makes them out to be) to keep his employees from becoming complacent and falling into administration mode.[3] Yet he inspires thousands of employees and millions of others because of his entrepreneurial mindset and vision. His employees feel like their work is meaningful, that they're making a difference. And they are. Because they follow an entrepreneurial leader.

Although Jobs and Musk have inspired others to the point of extreme emulation,[4] most people have learned the wrong lessons from them. It's tough to learn the right lessons when we're all stuck in a paradigm of administration—an *administration ethos*, if you will.

In this chapter, we'll perform a deep diagnosis of the problem—the cause of the prevalence of administration mode, the root of the administration ethos that pervades the world. We point the finger at universities, which have become deeply administrative—not just in organization and operation but in their very culture and ethos. It is no wonder that the graduates they produce enter the business world in full-fledged administration mode.

WHY ARE THERE SO FEW ENTREPRENEURIAL LEADERS AMONG MBA'S?

The problem that we need to diagnose is this: There's much too small a supply of entrepreneurial leaders for the demand. *All* businesses need an entrepreneurial leader at their top to get and stay in venture mode. Really, they need entrepreneurial leaders throughout their organization, but especially at the top.

Everyone is *looking* for an entrepreneurial leader—their own Steve Jobs. But there are just so few that the vast majority of businesses have none at all.[5] This supply shortage of entrepreneurial leaders turns our attention, once again, to business education, which *should* be the training ground for such business leaders.

But universities suppress the spirit of entrepreneurial leadership with their curriculum and the professors who teach it and too often demand concordance to their unchallenged views. Critical thinking, challenging assumptions, and innovative thinking are not only left untaught—they're actively quelled.

This wasn't always the case. For centuries, universities were places of active debate and insight. What happened to universities that has rendered them mass producers of, at best, administrators and, at worst, mindless drones?

THE RISE OF THE ADMINISTRATION ETHOS

The express aim of universities is to train their students for employment, whatever career path they choose. In a 2011 speech, former

University of Pennsylvania President Amy Gutmann confirmed this purpose when she celebrated employment data for graduates:

> Almost 90% of young college graduates were employed in 2010, compared with only 64% of their peers who did not attend college. . . . [C]ollege graduates are making on average almost double the annual earnings of those with only a high school diploma. And this advantage is likely to stick with them over a lifetime of work.[6]

She continued, "Even in the depths of the Great Recession, the unemployment rate of college graduates was less than half that of high school graduates, and never exceeded 5.1%."[7]

These are compelling arguments, although new research throws the cited data into question.[8] But that's beside the point. The goal of the brilliant and ambitious shouldn't be employment with a padded salary and benefits. They can create so much more value if they think bigger than just working for someone else, letting someone else figure out what problems to solve and, probably, even how to solve them. Smart and talented people can do administrative tasks and grunt work better than the average person. But is that really the best use of their gifts?

But Gutmann's view has the zeitgeist. Most of the world's smartest people choose to work for others. We get it. Entrepreneurial leadership isn't for everyone. It's a lot of work. It's uncertain. It's challenging. It's risky. You can have a great life under the security blanket of salaried managerial employment, riding the successes of someone else's entrepreneurial risk taking. We're not judging.

Gutmann's arguments constitute the fundamental transactional value proposition of universities: Students expect a job when they finish.

College as a Hotbed of Administration

The US remains culturally the most entrepreneurial in the world. The "American dream" remains, to a greater extent than most anywhere else in the world, an entrepreneurial one. Yet even in the US the culture has, to a significant extent, turned administrative. Youth are asked from a very young age what they want to *be* when they grow up, as in which established career position they want to occupy once they are adults. The more enterprising children will aspire to be some sort of explorer, like an inventor or an astronaut. But most—particularly as they approach the college years—are coached into wanting a safe, stable career that fits their talents.

This imbibing of the administration ethos only increases as young adults enter college. Students are told to figure out what degree and, thus, what career to pursue. And as a career preparator, the university and its administrators seek to shepherd enrollees into the career trajectories that the school has designed curricula to teach.

It's true that the term *entrepreneurship* can be found in the university curriculum in recent decades. The majority of universities now offer some entrepreneurship classes, many offer a minor degree in entrepreneurship, and a growing number of them even offer it as a business major. There's demand for these classes—not all bright university students want a safe, stable employment career. Some have bigger dreams.

But even these classes are, almost without fail, designed within administration mode—they teach *administrative* entrepreneurship! That's an oxymoron, of course. But the textbook approach to entrepreneurship education is a "scientific" approach based on the latest and greatest of entrepreneurship research. How do you build an effective team? How do you design your new organization? How do you maximize your chances of obtaining funding? What makes a winning pitch? Even creativity, innovation, and design are studied and taught "scientifically."

In short, the ethos in universities is an administration ethos—students are taught to follow a checklist of how to do whatever they need to do the "right" way. This administration ethos manifests in various ways in universities. Two of the more important manifestations of it pertain to doctrines espoused by the majority of academic faculty: technocracy and rationality. And, because academia is held up as a beacon of the best knowledge and thought in society, these doctrines have also permeated social and political thought.

The Persistent Faith in Technocracy

One of the primary barriers to an entrepreneurial mindset has been the faulty scientific and cultural paradigm of *technocracy*, which means, essentially, rule by science. To this day, many people expect science, AI, and benevolent political authorities to rule the world in such a way as to optimize total human welfare, bringing fairness, equity, and efficiency to the global economic order.

It's a fanciful utopian vision. Technocracy *doesn't work*. In fact, for reasons that economists have emphasized for over a century, it *can't* work. Why not?

Because the economy isn't a machine; nor its constituents mindless pawns to be moved at a technocrat's whims. The economy is *us*. It's our efforts to make the best lives for ourselves and our loved ones through our own productive efforts. We can't make our best lives when someone else is directing our every move. Our lives are endless journeys of discovery as we try to figure out how to become our best selves and live our best lives. Well-being is *self-actualized*. It's an absurd proposition, then, that some technocratic administrator could possibly know and dictate what sort of lives we ought to live.

The dream of technocracy has been founded on the presumption that human beings are all essentially the same, so there's a scientific formula for optimized human existence that works the same for every person. But that just isn't the case. We're *different*; we want and value different things; we love different things and people; we enjoy different lifestyles. How can a technocrat choose for you what you should have and what you should do?

In fact, the problem of technocracy goes even deeper than this. Even if the technocrat could somehow assign us jobs that we liked, technocracy would still fail because, again, the economy isn't a machine. It's a flow of information and knowledge. It's an evolving process of what people think and know, what they want, what they do and produce, what problems they run into, and why. How could a central planner possibly have the knowledge and information to direct productive activities effectively? The ambitions of certain political leaders to do so have led to disaster *every single time*.

History shows that one of the most important problems with technocracy is the absence of entrepreneurs—those who provide different knowledge and understanding of what people want and need. Entrepreneurs put their knowledge of all sorts of people and things to use in new and creative ways that could never be foreseen by any technocrat. Technocracy is essentially a *ban* on entrepreneurship. It is total governance by administration.

Entrepreneurs are the health of a growing economy, the engine of economic growth. We need *more* entrepreneurs, not fewer. We need *fewer* administrators, not more. We need people who aspire to new value creation, not to administration (e.g., political office).

But academia is replete with technocracy advocates. Historians predominantly celebrate the "great leaders" of expansive government administration while deriding the great entrepreneurs of the past as, e.g., "robber barons." Psychologists and sociologists have written endlessly on how we should design better institutions to create a better, fairer society. Even a lot of economists see the economy as a machine to be controlled, using policy levers to engineer greater productivity and equality.

For some of the greatest of scholarly minds, great knowledge and expertise reveal to them just how little we actually know and can predict or design. Most academics, however, don't seem to reach that level of deep knowledge that engenders such epistemic humility. Instead, they're supercilious mediocrities, ignorant of their own ignorance. They are the primary proponents of administration.

The Myth of Rationality

The second core academic myth underpinning the administration ethos is the myth of human *rationality.* Humans, it is supposed, are generally rational, self-interested creatures.

Now, many have since figured out that this isn't entirely or always true. Psychologists have studied the propensity for humans to make cognitive errors in their decisions. Common biases and heuristics affect our decisions and render us occasionally "irrational" creatures. Renowned scholars in this vein have published best-selling books about what we can do to avoid such errors, with solutions ranging from personal advice to policy prescriptions. Underneath it all is a presumption that rationality is the goal—that we want to optimize our behavior. And that we *can.* We just need a little help to get over our biases and see reality more objectively. Again, cue our benevolent technocratic overlords.

But what's interesting is that this whole idea and pursuit of human rationality is and has always been a *myth*, a misguided vestige of the administration ethos and its relentlessly technocratic pursuit of scientific optimization.

Human beings aren't rational. We're not even "predictably irrational." There's just no such thing as human rationality in the majority of human decision-making and conduct. We're thoughtful. We're imaginative. We can be instinctive or deliberate. But we aren't "rational," at least not in the generally understood sense that we "maximize our utility."

The concept of rationality is premised upon a supposition that there's some *optimum*, an action that is ideal, that maximizes utility. Hidden underneath this assumption is an implied rejection of entrepreneurship—that what already exists is all there is.

Think about it like this: For there to be a *best* option, there has to be a finite set of options, each of which has a known outcome (or, at least, a known probability distribution of known possible outcomes). But is that true? Almost never. You always have more options. In fact, you always have *endless* options. You just have to imagine them. And you never really know what the possible outcomes are. Believing you do is one of the most *un*entrepreneurial mindsets that there is. Any experienced entrepreneur knows that surprises are inevitable—and frequent.

But this narrow, constrained, unentrepreneurial rationality myth dominates the behavioral sciences. It's a social engineering mindset—a dogma that we can build a better world by figuring out how and why people make choices we don't like and engineering a way to prompt them to choose better. This behavioral paradigm has failed utterly, but scholars still cling to their faith in its precepts as the evidence mounts of its abysmal predictive or corrective power.

It turns out that *we can't know why* people do what they do. Sometimes we ourselves aren't particularly clear on why we do what we do. Sometimes people do things impulsively because it seems right or fun in the moment. It turns out, people don't actually deliberate on many of their choices. Most choices are made on impulse—what to wear, what to have for breakfast, which way to walk, etc. People don't carefully examine all the options available and map out their respective utilities so as to optimize their choice. They just pick an option that feels right and go with it.

The myth of rationality bolsters expectations that the world can (and should) be administrated. It's completely false. But it's the foundation of the business school, where the curriculum is fundamentally premised on the myth of rationality.

By teaching administration and instilling what is too often thought of as a revered "scientific" approach to decision-making, students learn to use decision tools and checklists to maximize their outcomes. The problem is how this way of making decisions constrains the entrepreneurial mind. It teaches students to look for the most rational choice within the set of existing and familiar options. The possibility of rethinking *beyond* that which already exists—how things are already done, how goals or outcomes are usually achieved—is undermined.

There is extensive research on human creativity, and still to date, there is very little that we really understand about how the mind creatively innovates. But one thing that is absolutely crystal clear from creativity research is that the creative mind can become easily *constrained* by finite-set thinking. As soon as people assume that the set of options available is fixed, no mental energy is given to possibilities outside that set.

In short, the myth of rationality taught in universities makes students *less* entrepreneurial. This sets them up well enough for administrative positions in the lower and middle levels of management. But it makes them terrible business leaders.

The Root of the Administration Ethos

Let's dig a bit deeper to expose the real root of the issue. It's tempting to blame government for it—there is no organization more representative of administration mode than a government organization. But while bureaucratic government administration deeply affects our lives, it has a lighter touch on how we *think*. If anything, most of us see government administration as a shining example of what not to do in business. No, the government isn't the real root of our administration ethos, although it shares plenty of blame. The root cause lies in the universities.

How and why have universities become such hotbeds of administration?

Universities are, for the most part, nonmarket organizations. As a consequence, they're undisciplined by both the profit motive and by competition. Private, for-profit schools are, to some limited extent, an exception. But even private schools conform to the industry norms and standards set by public and nonprofit universities.

One key factor is the lack of competition in the higher education industry. Universities have competition, of course, but not really. They compete for students, sort of. But the supply of prospective students is plenty sufficient that all major universities get their fill. They just compete for the *best* students, which helps with their rankings and, if lucky, with their fundraising (in the long run). So you'll see schools try to woo students with gamed rankings, beautiful campuses, athletic programs, entertainment options, and other amenities that give students "the college experience."

But, with very few exceptions, they're *not really* competing on education. To the contrary, virtually every university conforms its curricula to industry norms and standards. In fact, they *have to* because of the accreditation machine, which we'll explain shortly. So education doesn't advance in the same way that innovative industries do. It's stagnant, shielded from the burden of making constant improvements and innovation.

Another root cause of university administration is the conflation of the customer. Who is the university's (paying) customer? Instinctively, it's tempting to say it's the students (or, perhaps, their parents). But are they?

According to Bellwether, most universities are funded primarily by the government.[9] Public US universities receive substantial funding from the *state* in which they operate, which accounts for about a fourth of their total funding. The federal government provides another fifth or so of total revenues through its student aid, research grants, and other institutional support funding.

Community colleges are also sponsored by local municipalities. Some schools, like the Ivies and some public schools, have extremely large endowments, which produce interest payments large enough to fund many of their operations. Yet even these receive substantial financial support from the government. Tuition accounts for only about a sixth of all funding, and the extra fees (textbooks, testing services, gym memberships, etc.) account for another fourth of the budget.

In other words, students are a secondary customer. It seems the real customer is the government. Even the bulk of tuition revenues are paid for by the federal government's student loan programs.

We can clearly see, once this is taken in, that universities have become instruments to achieve political goals. They train students to accept a particular political ideology. What they think and teach is shaped by state funding. Federal and state research grants go to scholars on the basis of their projects' accordance with political goals rather than on the scientific or economic merits of the project. Grant monies flow to politically favored projects, which severely distorts the marketplace of ideas. The money attracts research interest, not the other way around, and "scientific" consensuses collate where the grant funding goes. Grant recipients gain instant academic prestige but are also vastly more likely to get their research published—not necessarily because their research is better, but simply because it is *funded* and, therefore, can be completed.

Unfunded research is hard to do in many disciplines because it requires expensive equipment or hired help. So grant recipients get published, obtain editorial positions at prestigious academic journals, and have a disproportionate amount of influence on their disciplines. In this way, grant funders, in turn, have an inordinate amount of influence on academic disciplines. And because the state is the biggest funder of grants, political motivations severely shape the academic landscape.

If you ask academics why academia has such an ideological slant, many will tell you it's because their ideas are more correct and have won the day in the scientific process. Hardly. Instead, many of the prevailing theories are shielded from challenge, as heterodox challengers are dismissed and derided without serious debate.

The orthodoxy gets its justification from the consensus of the orthodoxy, and not from producing superior arguments.[10] "The science is settled" is an utterly unscientific and even antiscientific claim. In fact, the research shows that many of those who subscribe to the dominant ideology, including academics, can't even articulate the arguments from the other side.[11] They don't need to.

This ideological tilt in universities is the climate in which students are trained. There's no debate. Students who question their professors on controversial topics can find themselves in hot water. Students who don't readily imbibe the dogma learn to say what's expected of them and keep their heads down. Ideas aren't challenged; critical thinking isn't developed. It's the opposite. University campuses have become dangerous places to explore new ideas.

Compounding this are the strings attached to state and federal funds that universities accept. These rules and regulations generate additional layers of bureaucracy. Universities employ teams of compliance officers who put in place, monitor, and enforce rules for university faculty and administration in order to comply with the rules attached to government funds. Again, these strings are often politically motivated, pushing schools toward accomplishing political ends.

Few organizations are as bureaucratic and inefficient as universities because of their administration ethos. They are run by administrators who have built their own protections to shield themselves from criticism and reform. These protections generally entail bureaucratic regulations and requirements—hoops that students and faculty must jump through, not because such steps are actually necessary but because they ensure the administration has enough work to do to justify its existence.

Universities are among the *least* entrepreneurial organizations in the world. They don't embrace entrepreneurial leadership—in fact, they mostly despise it. And, with the exception of a few great (but radical) professors, they don't teach it.

THE ACCREDITATION MACHINE

One core reason—perhaps the biggest reason—why the administration ethos has taken such root within universities and why bureaucracy runs amok within the higher education system is the accreditation process, which merits deeper treatment.

Arguably, the reason administration mode is so pervasive in universities and B-schools is they're *designed* to be that way—universities are *required* to run this way, to teach this way. These are the requirements of the accrediting bodies that grant universities their legitimacy and status.

The goal of accreditation seems valid on the surface. According to the US Department of Education, "Accreditation ensures that institutions of higher education meet acceptable levels of quality."[12] Accrediting agencies, officially recognized and approved by the government, assess the operations and curricula of university systems to ensure that they meet normal operational standards and that the content the university teaches is accepted as scientific and rigorous.

There are two types of accreditation: institutional and programmatic. Institutional accreditation establishes the legitimacy of the university as a whole. Programmatic accreditation, as its name suggests, accredits specific colleges or programs offered typically within some university system.

Verifying standards is the Department of Education's stated number one function for accreditation. They tell students which institutions are "acceptable." They direct public and private investments to compliant universities. And they protect accredited schools from "harmful internal and external pressure."[13]

In other words, accreditors hold the reins over which schools get funding and students and which don't. Accreditation makes it *necessary* to conform to normal standards.

First, an accreditation agency establishes standards. How do they decide what the standards should be? Well, essentially they look at what the top schools are doing. They're the top schools, so they must be doing it best, right? They are the standard.

Second, a team of accreditors, usually constituted of respected academics such as deans of other accredited schools, attends a peer institution to audit their processes and compare them to the "best practice" standards that they've predetermined. This means that all schools are patterned, virtually identically, after each other. Perhaps more accurately, virtually all schools are patterned after the top schools, the ones who are deemed the standard. There is some room for deviation, a little bit of innovation, but it's extremely limited.

If you don't comply, you are condemned to be an unaccredited school—buyer beware. There are some schools that have survived without accreditation. But it's tough. Accreditation is, again, the key to obtaining funding, attracting students, and avoiding harmful pressures.

The Consequences of Accreditation

What does this mean for universities? It means that, at most, a very small subset of all universities are innovating. Innovation is risky. Innovation might cause the school to fail accreditation. Conformity is safe. Conformity grants the school legitimacy.

It's the logic of administration mode. In order to get that invaluable stamp of approval, schools have to become bureaucracies. Bureaucracy is baked into the process of accreditation, which is a primary reason why the university system hasn't changed substantively in centuries.

What if, heaven forbid, the orthodoxy has it *wrong*? Professor Roger Koppl calls this "expert failure" and warns that professional standardization organizations, like university accreditation agencies, ensure that expert failures are distributed far and wide and have vast and consequential effects.[14] The system also ensures that the failures are not corrected for a very, very long time.

AACSB

Business schools are accredited by the Association to Advance Collegiate Schools of Business, or AACSB. As of this writing, over one thousand business schools worldwide are accredited by the AACSB. According to the AACSB itself, "AACSB accreditation is recognized worldwide as the highest level of excellence a business school can achieve."[15]

"Earning AACSB accreditation," the AACSB further declares, "signifies a business school's commitment to strategic management, learner success, thought leadership, and societal impact."[16]

The AACSB's current standards were determined and formally adopted most recently in 2020. Early in 2025, they announced the formalization of a "global standard-setting framework" that would guide the AACSB "in developing, revising and maintaining its global standards, including the fundamental principles around standard-setting, and the due process steps involved when revisions occur."[17]

Again, the problem is how this completely elides the primary mechanisms that *we teach* in the business school as best practices for organizational discipline, innovation, and strategic management. It's an utterly *un*entrepreneurial approach to business education—it's business school education by administration. Which is, of course, precisely why it's an education *in* business administration.

WHERE CAN BUSINESSES LOOK FOR ENTREPRENEURIAL LEADERS?

We've argued that top-level business leaders need to act entrepreneurially and stay in *venture mode*. Yet universities, business schools in particular, actively nurture an administration mindset that renders students *less* entrepreneurial. As a result, business schools are a great place to hire administrators, but looking for entrepreneurial leaders among college graduates is like looking for a dime in a barrel of pennies.

Where, then, *can* we look for entrepreneurial leaders?

The answer lies in identifying the venture mindset rather than the educated administrator. Look for character rather than qualifications. There's no "identikit" picture, but here are some of the traits:

- **Empathic orientation:** Entrepreneurial leaders seek to be right in assessing end users' needs (How can I make this person's life better?) and not with spreadsheets or business abstractions.

- **Bold imagination:** Entrepreneurship begins with imagining new future value. Imaginativeness can't be taught (though it can be practiced), but it's possible to find people who already demonstrate aptitude.
- **Relentless iteration:** Entrepreneurs are not overcommitted to their initial idea but treat it as a hypothesis to be tested and refined based on feedback. They keep iterating propositions that customers *could* love until they find one that they *do* love.
- **Bias for action:** Venture mode elevates action over strategy and is driven by people who are doers, not planners. Whatever the uncertainty, entrepreneurs start by building (a mock-up, a prototype, a new workflow) and use this as a starting point from which to advance.
- **Systems thinking:** Administrators prefer linear cause-and-effect processes and controlled outcomes. Systems thinkers thrive on the nonlinearity of complexity and interconnectedness. They can imagine a new solution in its entirety before reverse-engineering it into reality.
- **Never-ending curiosity:** Venturers don't submit to administrative bosses who are afraid of pushing boundaries. They're never satisfied with "good enough." They explore. They're constantly reinventing.
- **Ownership mentality:** Not everyone is a founder, but venture mode employees and managers always exhibit an ownership mindset. They act like the business is theirs, even if it isn't. They don't wait for orders but step up when needed. They hate waste.
- **Anti-bureaucratic instinct:** Venturers bristle at red tape and regulation. They don't see "we've always done it this way" as a good reason. They dismantle obstacles to

> progress without first asking for permission. They have a disdain for administrative bloat and useless reports.

Most organizations tend to look at middle management (promotion from within) or at rival firms (external hires) for new leaders. The intuition regarding these is strong. They have industry experience. They know how the business works. They have management experience. But their management experience is most likely *administrative* and not entrepreneurial. This is why most businesses find themselves in administration mode eventually. Can entrepreneurial leaders be found among the ranks of middle management? Sometimes.

Microsoft, for example, found Satya Nadella inside their organization. He'd been an internal leader focused on applying newly emerging principles and practices of agile business methodology—a highly entrepreneurial role. But such leaders are hard to spot because good performance as a middle manager tends to be more about administrative leadership (making the numbers) than it is about entrepreneurial leadership.

As for MBAs, they're simply untrained and unprepared for such entrepreneurial leadership, especially at the top levels. They'll need to build entrepreneurial leadership experience—whether by founding their own company or by working their way up the management ranks (while somehow avoiding the enticing fall into administration mode). Mostly, they need the administrative mindset drubbed out of them before they can switch to venture mode.

Note that, although entrepreneurial leaders are scarce, the problem of scarcity isn't an inherent market failure. There's no innate reason why there can't be more entrepreneurial leaders. But the current market is underproducing them and overproducing administrators.

NEW APPROACHES

We're not the first to diagnose this problem and point the finger at universities. And there have been some limited efforts to take a different tack. For example, Peter Thiel, (co)founder of PayPal, Palantir, and Founders Fund, has understood the problem of the administration ethos nurtured in universities for a while.

Ever one to take entrepreneurial action, he created the highly controversial Thiel Fellowship, where ambitious youth can "skip or stop out of college to receive a $100,000 grant"[18] to join a two-year program designed specifically to nurture an entrepreneurial mind. In fact, university students *must* drop out in order to accept the fellowship.

On its website, the Thiel Fellowship program explains,

> College can be good for learning about what's been done before, but it can also discourage you from doing something new. Each of our fellows charts a unique course; together they have proven that young people can succeed by thinking for themselves instead of following a traditional track and competing on old career tracks.[19]

The Thiel Fellowship, among other radical approaches, illustrates a growing entrepreneurial anxiety toward traditional education, in both high school and university, and an innovative search for alternatives.

Rethink the System

Universities have become fountains of administrators, fabricating graduates who think and do as taught in the "most correct and best" way. Do not question. Questioning "The Science®" is expressly verboten. To disagree with the scientific consensus is to presume expertise beyond the best and brightest who have studied an issue.

Of course, questioning established norms and beliefs is the foundation of the entrepreneurial mindset needed for venture mode and entrepreneurial leadership. When you produce obedient drones, you get obeisant employees and administrators. What you don't get are entrepreneurial leaders.

There are plenty of entrepreneurs that come from the university ranks. But the vast majority of this select bunch build an entrepreneurial mindset *despite* their university training and not *because* of it. They were trained for employment. But when you get tens of thousands of very bright people passing through your ranks, at least a few of them will end up being too ambitious to work for someone else.

This is why you see established and successful entrepreneurial leaders—people like Peter Thiel and Marc Andreessen—question the value of a university education. It's not that the education is worthless. It's actually worse than that. Universities kill the entrepreneurial mindset. They overproduce administrators and underproduce entrepreneurial leaders. It's past time to rethink this system.

CHAPTER 9

CAN ENTREPRENEURSHIP BE TAUGHT?

In the prior chapter, we argued that universities, generally, and business schools, specifically, instill in their graduates an administrative mindset, the adversary and antithesis of venture mode, and effectively preclude the possibility of students developing an entrepreneurial mindset. This is an economic tragedy since entrepreneurship is the fuel for all economic growth and for the value creation approach to business management that we call venture mode.

Does it have to be this way? Can education be reformed in such a way to teach and nurture entrepreneurial leadership?

Some have argued—persuasively—that entrepreneurial leadership can't be taught. In a particularly interesting debate in 2012,[1] Noam Wasserman[2] argued that entrepreneurship is a skill little different from other trained professions, such as accounting, engineering, medicine, or law.

Victor Hwang,[3] on the other side of the debate, argued that real entrepreneurship is just too messy and bears too little semblance to the idealistic versions taught in the classroom. "Leading a start-up," he noted, "demands a deep understanding of people that can only come from real-world experience."[4]

Tim Askew, founder of sales and consulting firm Corporate Rain International, added his own skepticism of entrepreneurial education:

> You can and should study everything in that [entrepreneurial] quest: from physics, to poetry, to philosophy, to history, to economics, to biology. Study anything and everything. Except entrepreneurship.[5]

This idea that the entrepreneurial mindset is either innate to us or else born out of life experience, that it can't be taught, is compelling. But it's wrong. Entrepreneurship *can* be taught, but not in the way its advocates, like Professor Wasserman, suppose. Critics of entrepreneurial education are very right that what's generally taught at business schools is not entrepreneurship—it's administration. Administrators might be able to run a small business quite effectively. But they're only "entrepreneurs" in a narrow and largely unhelpful sense. Teaching administrative entrepreneurship, if anything, makes people *poorer* entrepreneurial leaders because it teaches them to run their ventures in administration mode.

TEACHING ADMINISTRATIVE ENTREPRENEURSHIP

In the prior chapter, we briefly observed that entrepreneurship is taught in universities from within the universities' administration ethos and that entrepreneurship is taught in *administration mode*. Let's elaborate on that argument here because it's important.

The prevailing entrepreneurship education paradigm, the one that virtually all entrepreneurship textbooks are based on, is that same positivist scientific paradigm that we discussed in chapter three, which permeates universities worldwide, as we discussed in chapter eight. The presumption of most entrepreneurship scholars is that the goal of entrepreneurship research is to unravel the secrets of successful entrepreneurship: What makes for a good pitch to investors? What does a good founding team look like? How should ventures be organized? Or, how can larger companies organize to achieve an "entrepreneurial orientation"? And of course, why do some ventures succeed while others fail? What are the main and common differences between successes and failures?

These broad research questions have been explored for decades now. Entrepreneurship data is messy, but we've found several statistical relationships that scholars have presumed to be clear evidence of causal relationships. For example, a meta-analysis of studies on the link between an entrepreneur's personality and venture performance concluded that "conscientiousness, openness to experience, emotional stability, and extraversion are each positively related to entrepreneurial firm performance."[6] In another review, scholars assessed the benefits of education on entrepreneurship performance and found "the effect of education on performance is positive and significant."[7]

It's within this paradigm that we find Professor Wasserman making his case. The accumulation of statistical evidence can, arguably, instruct prospective entrepreneurs on what characteristics, approaches, etc. of ventures are most likely to succeed. As he put it in the debate, "We can teach founders to use [data] to avoid common hazards."[8]

Professor Wasserman's view is highly representative of the typical academic view of entrepreneurship as a *scientific* (or, more accurately, "scientistic"[9]) endeavor, born out of universities' administration ethos. There is, as understood within the universities' administration ethos, a scientific optimum—a best approach to all things. Even entrepreneurship.

In fact, one of the leading strands of entrepreneurial studies to emerge in recent years is the "theory-based view," which promotes a "scientific method for startups."[10] In this view, entrepreneurs are understood essentially as scientists who develop economic value hypotheses and test them.[11] If this is correct, then entrepreneurs can certainly be instructed in the scientific method and how to perform rigorous hypothesis testing. Not all hypotheses will prove correct, but through rigorous testing, these can be weeded out quickly and efficiently, making way for those that succeed in market testing.

This view is appealing. But it's wrong. It's an administrative approach to entrepreneurship. In entrepreneurship, administration is constrictive, inhibiting the exploration of new and expansive value creation that's required for venture growth. Entrepreneurship can only really be effective in venture mode.

CAN ADMINISTRATIVE ENTREPRENEURS GO ROGUE?

An important conceptual distinction that Mark has made in his research (with coauthors Russ McBride and Brent Clark) is between *conforming entrepreneurship* and *rogue entrepreneurship*.[12] Conforming entrepreneurship generally involves replicating a familiar value proposition. It's opening another fast-food franchise, a new laundromat, another accounting firm.

The value of these ventures is established and familiar. When you pitch the idea to others, they all get it. They know and understand what the value is. For these sorts of ventures, demand is already largely established and, so, can be estimated. This allows entrepreneurs to crunch the numbers to assess the expected ROI.

But *rogue entrepreneurship* is different. These are the entrepreneurs who buck norms and introduce something different, something unexpected. These are the Steve Jobses who ignored the prevailing expert sentiment—expressed by Ken Olson, CEO of Digital Equipment Inc., who in 1977 said, "There is no reason anyone would want a computer in their home." The rogue entrepreneur looks at the experts, the influencers, and indeed most people, who all say the same thing—*You're crazy, that would never work*—and responds, *You're wrong. Just watch.*

Rogue entrepreneurs include Travis Kalanick, cofounder of Uber, who bet on disrupting the taxi industry with a smartphone app and ride-sharers. And Lamar Hunt, who started the AFL as a rival to the NFL, brought in new rules to make the games more high-scoring and entertaining, and merged it into the NFL to create the world's most successful sports league. And Gary Dahl, who convinced millions to buy a rock as a pet.[13] And Elon Musk, who, seeing the trajectory of humanity, determined that the future will require mankind to become interplanetary. Many people would hear Musk's claim that we have to terraform Mars as the rantings of a lunatic. We'll see.

A scientific approach to entrepreneurship would have rendered a rejection of each of those entrepreneurial hypotheses. The general consensus—what we call in our research the *assessment context*—renders a judgment that these ideas are bad, that there's no demand for them. And strictly speaking, that conclusion is correct—demand didn't yet exist for such ideas.

But rogue entrepreneurs are the epitome of entrepreneurial leadership.

They earn admiration for their rejection of a scientific, administrative approach, ignoring market data and evidence, instead imagining a new and different vision for a better future and then setting out to create it. The lack of existing demand is not a problem for entrepreneurial leaders—they just need to change people's minds. And they do. Because their vision is compelling. Because they're persuasive. But most importantly, because they're *right*.

Not all rogue entrepreneurs prove to be entrepreneurial leaders. Many of them fail, sometimes spectacularly. And not everything that entrepreneurial leaders touch always turns to gold. Entrepreneurial leaders fail when their vision ultimately proves technologically impossible or else uncompelling to most.

But entrepreneurial leaders often win despite the jeering skepticism of other experts because they have a vision of a better future—not for themselves but for their customers. They understand their customers on a deep level—deeper, sometimes, even than they understand themselves. They see the future through a lens that others don't (or can't), at least not yet. But they inspire others to see and choose the future they envision over the status quo.

This is what Steve Jobs meant when he said,

> Some people say, "Give the customers what they want." But that's not my approach. Our job is to figure out what they're going to want before they do. I think Henry Ford once said, "If I'd asked customers what they wanted, they would have told me, 'A faster horse!'" People don't know what they want until you show it to them. That's why I never rely on market research. Our task is to read things that are not yet on the page.[14]

TEACHING THE TOOLS OF ENTREPRENEURSHIP

If we're right, and entrepreneurial leadership *can* be taught or, at least, nurtured, then what would such an education look like? We'll go into specifics of what an entrepreneurial education system might look like in the next chapter, but here let's discuss the *content* of such an education. What, if anything, can be actually taught?

Entrepreneurial leadership is, again, about entrepreneurial vision, as well as an insatiable drive to make the vision a reality. Entrepreneurial leaders imagine a unique and viable future that outshines other possible futures and then turn reality's course so that the imagined future is the one that comes about. They enlist others into this vision, showing how "this is the right way," and break through cognitive and technological barriers to reach that possible future.

Mutual friend and mentor Peter Klein likens entrepreneurship to art. One can be taught the tools and techniques of art. They can be practiced and developed. But one can't really be taught what art *is*, what makes it *good* art, or *how* to be a good artist. This is essentially true of entrepreneurship also. Entrepreneurial vision can't really be taught, just as artistic vision can't be. But there *are* principles, mindsets, approaches, tools, and techniques that can be used to understand consumers' needs, build usable designs, develop a compelling pitch deck, organize effectively, etc.

Wil Schroter, founder and CEO of Startups.com, put it well:

> The focus for entrepreneurial education should not be about "making people entrepreneurs," it should be about equipping prospective entrepreneurs with as many useful tools as possible for their upcoming journey.[15]

The key set of tools necessary for entrepreneurship includes *empathy*, *ingenuity*, *judgment*, and *tenacity*. Not a single one of these can be taught in a formulaic fashion. Scientific study of each of these has rendered mostly confusion and debate. This isn't to say that we've learned nothing—we've learned quite a lot. But what we haven't been able to figure out is exactly where these skills come from or how they're developed.

Much worse, many of the attempts to study the use of entrepreneurial skill sets in behavioral science have been what scholars have called "as-if" theorizing: the use of overly simplistic and admittedly false models that (superficially) predict well. That is, we behave *as if* this were how we actually think.[16] These models, fit to past data, seem to explain so much. But they end up performing terribly in reality (they have a terrible track record of prediction) because they don't actually reflect what's really going on. So when the past doesn't repeat, as is inevitable, the model invariably fails.

These as-if models are examples of the "scientism" that Hayek talked about.[17] They give a false sense of scientific rigor and precision to what is, in fact, clunky and simplistic theorizing. But these clunky models are the core of the university curricula.

The myth of rationality that we discussed in the previous chapter, for example, is representative of as-if theory. Treating humans *as if* we were rational allows the development of predictive models. Of course, when real human agents don't behave as predicted by the model, they call the actual behavior "biased" and "irrational," leaving the underlying theory of rationality intact.

Of course people don't actually make decisions like a calculator. On the rare occasions they do deliberate carefully over a decision (e.g., a big purchase like a home or a car), it's almost never a thorough utility maximization calculus. Instead, people consider their options and determine which of them they *want most.*

There has been, with a few exceptions, very little curiosity among behavioral scholars toward a better descriptive understanding of how human minds *actually* make these judgments, i.e., how people actually decide in a moment what they want. The as-if model has taken hold as the theoretic paradigm, and descriptive analysis of human judgment has been shaped by and within this paradigm, even though it's not at all how people a*ctually* make decisions.

When universities teach decision-making, they teach to the as-if model. They teach how to maximize utility. They teach students how to recognize their biases and account for them in the calculus. But since the model isn't representative of how people *actually* make decisions, it's practically useless, particularly when it comes to adventurous possibilities like rogue entrepreneurship. There's no maximization of anything in rogue entrepreneurship. Rogue entrepreneurs are navigating uncharted waters—there's no *best path* through uncharted terrain. Adventurers can't choose their path with a calculator.

Once we turn our attention away from as-if models and toward description of what actually happens, the tools we can develop to aid entrepreneurs suddenly become much more promising and efficacious. Here is a brief overview of some of what *can* be taught.

Developing Empathy

The first core principle of entrepreneurial leadership, necessary for unlocking venture mode, is empathy. Or, to put it more specifically, *entrepreneurial empathy*. Entrepreneurial empathy is the capacity to understand the needs and wants of consumers. Entrepreneurial vision is necessarily centered on a problem to solve—specifically, an *unmet consumer need*. A good way to think about an unmet need is as dissatisfaction—wanting some experience to be better. In actuality, no one is ever perfectly satisfied. Even the most content among us knows that life could be better, easier, more enjoyable. It's the human condition to want improvement.

Entrepreneurship—value creation—is about solving the problem of dissatisfaction better than ever before. It's about better satisfying people's persistently unmet needs, doing jobs that people need done better. And these services and products are *valuable* to the extent that they contribute to making people's lives better. This is equally true for business-to-business customers as it is for end users.

But to do this, entrepreneurs must *understand* consumers' problems in a way that hasn't been fully grasped before. They must understand other people's experiences, their needs, in a profound way. You can't just ask customers what their needs are. Most likely, *they don't know them* or, at least, they can't clearly articulate them.

People aren't born with an innate sense of exactly what they need. All we experience is what economist Ludwig von Mises called "uneasiness,"[18] which is always internalized (and communicated) with some degree of vagueness and imprecision. To get into venture mode, entrepreneurial leaders have to try to infer from these vaguely expressed experiences of uneasiness a specific way to resolve them. Uneasy people have learned ways to get by with what they've got now. But they don't know what to want *next*.

Of course, *some* people can express frustrations with the current solutions. These frustrations are huge clues into what their needs really are. Bill Gates wrote, "Unhappy customers are always a concern. They're also your greatest opportunity. Adopting a learning posture rather than a negative defensive posture can make customer complaints your best source of significant quality improvements."[19] This is absolutely true. If your customers are unhappy with your solution, it's inevitably because there's a discrepancy between the expectation they were sold and the value you actually delivered. Whatever the reason, you need to learn from these dissatisfied customers and do better.

But, as Steve Jobs famously remarked, most people don't know what they want until you show it to them. This includes frustrated, dissatisfied customers. They might be able to tell you what didn't work for them. They might even be able to tell you what they want. But what they can tell you they want is almost never what they *should* want because they're almost never in a position to know what that should be. They just don't have the technological expertise, or even a sufficient grasp of their needs, to do so. What they say they want might be an improvement over what you've created so these suggestions are worth listening to. But it's the *entrepreneur's* job to figure out better solutions to consumers' needs—to bring cutting-edge knowledge to bear on consumers' needs experiences.

So how can *you* know what consumers will want in the future? Empathy is the cognitive process by which we understand other people. Empathy is a critical factor for entrepreneurship, the crucial process needed to turn venture mode on. If you're not good at empathy, you'll have a difficult time coming up with a great idea or knowing if the idea's great.

But empathy *can* be learned, at least partially. It's knowledge based, and there are methods to empathically use knowledge about others to create a mental model of how those others think about and experience their needs. Spend time with your customers. Watch them. Talk to them. Don't give them surveys or ask them to leave a review, have a conversation with them. Put yourself in their life and learn how they live it. And through this learning, you can come to a better entrepreneurial vision of a better future for them, and for all.[20]

Improving Judgment

A second necessary skill for entrepreneurship is *entrepreneurial judgment*. Again, like empathy, this is a skill that can be trained and honed, but it's not a skill that can be applied formulaically. It's not a skill that AI can reproduce.

Most people think of judgment as decision-making. But entrepreneurship scholars distinguish between the two. Decision-making is picking the best choice from a set of options. It's *choosing*. The choices considered are those that are familiar—people choose from what they already know. This is administration mode.

Judgment, however, involves figuring out what to do when there is no given set of options—the possibilities are quite literally endless.

Entrepreneurially minded people don't confine themselves to the known and familiar. They look for options outside of the familiar, searching for something new and different. Something better. Something unique. Never tried before. Perhaps never contemplated before.

Of course, sometimes they want something familiar, something they really like—their favorites. We all do. But entrepreneurs keep the "new and different" option on the table and enjoy choosing it regularly.

Of course, virtually all the tools that behavioral scientists have developed are tools for *decision-making* and not for judgment. The vast majority of behavioral scientists don't distinguish between them. As far as they can tell, judgment is essentially the same as decision-making—in judgment, we just know a little less about the probabilities of the options and their corresponding outcomes.

But that's not right. As economist Frank Knight famously explained, for judgment *there are no probabilities*; they don't exist. Probabilities only exist when you have a known and closed set of options and outcomes. In judgment, you don't have that, so there are no probabilities. Economist G. L. S. Shackle suggested that we abandon the language of probability for judgment, which is false and misleading, and replace it with the language of *possibility*. We agree.

When business students learn decision-making in their classes, they're taught how to maximize expected utility. They're taught how to avoid common biases and use data to scientifically inform their choice, often against their intuition. These skills and tools are great if you're in a stable, predictable industry. But stable, predictable industries aren't where the entrepreneurial profits are. These profits are in uncharted "blue oceans"[21]—market segments that are unbloodied by competition—uncharted waters where there's no stability or predictability. Decision-making in blue oceans using analytical tools and big data results in garbage. There simply are no existing, stable data to render a valid probabilistic result.

But entrepreneurial judgment *can* be improved with better instruction, with practice, and most importantly, with *wisdom*. Better entrepreneurial judgment entails a full and conscientious acknowledgment of what and how much we *don't and can't* know. Only in such acknowledgment can sound judgment be made to account for the possibilities that are unknowable *ex ante*. A big paradigm shift is required—away from the analytical decision-making approaches taught in business schools today to an informed but intuitive and experience-based judgment approach.

Promoting Ingenuity

Creativity and ingenuity are two more of the black boxes of venture mode that perpetually slip from the grasp of empirical science. These have been dubbed by scholars "the fuzzy front end"[22] of entrepreneurship due to large and persistent empirical knowledge gaps regarding the creative process—we just don't really understand where ideas come from.

The problem is that we can't see *inside* the mind to observe what is going on to lead to new ideas. Yes, we've learned some things, but studies of the brain using fMRI, EEG, ERP, and other neuroimaging tools have yielded surprisingly little real insight. In a 2010 review of the academic literature, researchers concluded that "creative thinking does not appear to critically depend on any single mental process or brain region, and it is not especially associated with right brains, defocused attention, low arousal, or alpha synchronization, as sometimes hypothesized."[23]

In other words, we just don't know *how* creativity works.

But we do know some other useful things about how minds work. For example, our minds categorize all things into *schemas*: categorical groupings of related concepts, rules (scripts), social roles, and other key ways of categorizing reality. For instance, if we start talking about college professors, a cognitive schema of professors is brought to mind. This schema encompasses what you know and think about professors—who they are (an "ideal type"), what they do (teaching, research, etc.), what they're like ("stereotypes"), and what their role is in society. We can't stop our minds from doing this categorization. It's what minds do.

When we search for new ideas, we look in the obvious places first—the schemas most associated with the problem we're trying to solve. And we look in the schemas that are largest—the areas we are most expert in. And if we *still* can't find a solution, we start sweeping the depths of our memory for ideas until we either finally find a solution or else give up.

But consider what this means. A humorous parable tells of a drunk who'd lost his keys and was searching for them near a lamppost in the park. A policeman, seeing the man, stopped and asked what he was looking for. Learning of the lost keys, the officer asks, "And you lost them around here?"

"Nah," came the response. "I'm pretty sure I lost them farther back in the park."

Confused, the officer asked, "So why are you looking for them here?"

"This is where the light is," was his response.

When we look for solutions, we start where the light is. If we find a solution there, we often stop our search. But what kind of ideas come from under the lamppost, i.e., within the obvious schemas? Almost always, these are incremental innovations, obvious solutions. Obvious solutions can be great, of course. But at the same time, you never get truly radical, game-changing ideas under the lamppost.

We can learn (and teach) to search beyond the lamppost. But creativity, the ability to see new patterns and create novel connections across disparate schemas, is not formulaic. It's a skill that everyone can and should develop with practice. But we rarely practice creativity in schools. Instead, schools actively squelch creativity and instill conformity, obedience, and an administrative mindset—a belief that there is a "right" or "best" answer to every problem.

There is no "right" or "best" answer in entrepreneurship—there's always an even better answer. An entrepreneurial mind is always searching beyond the lamppost for better.

Entrepreneurial Tenacity

The last of the four unteachable skills of entrepreneurs is tenacity or grit. This is probably the easiest to acknowledge as unteachable. But in this case, it can be trained much more than is commonly thought.

Tenacity or grit is defined as "perseverance and passion for long-term goals."[24] It's traditionally understood as a personal trait—innate to our individual makeup—that engenders "sustained allocation of goal-directed energy"[25] toward specific (particularly difficult) tasks. Recently, however, scholars have determined that grit is more of a skill than a trait. This suggests that tenacity might be taught or, at least, trained. Yet, research on the trainability of grit has so far produced only "mixed" results.[26]

Tenacity is inherently a response to *uncertainty*. When we don't know the outcome, we can become frustrated or even paralyzed.

Imagine you were on a transoceanic flight when the explosion of one of the engines opens a hole in the fuselage, and you find yourself sucked out into the open air. Miraculously, you survive the fall and hit the water below at just the right angle to avoid serious injury. But as you surface, grateful for the miracle of surviving the fall, you realize you have to swim to safety. But where? There's no land in sight.

How long does your grit last when your life is on the line? The answer will certainly be different for different people, but in all cases, it's *not very long*. It's hopeless.

Now, unbeknownst to you, there is a populated island only a few miles away. But you don't know that. Because of your ignorance, there's no way to know which way or how far you have to go. You could pick a direction and just swim, but you know you won't last long.

But let's now add a wrinkle: You spot seagulls in the distance. Those birds can only mean one thing: land.

Now what's your grit like? Are you able to muster swimming three, five, ten miles in the direction of those birds if you're confident there's land waiting? Maybe not all of us, but many of us can.

But tenacity is needed precisely *because* of uncertainty. If we didn't have uncertainty, there would be no worries, no difficulties. You would always know just what needs to be done at all times. But there would also be no entrepreneurial gains, no profits.[27] The only reason entrepreneurs can win big is because they're willing to bear uncertainties and take on risks that others aren't. That's why they have to be tenacious. It's not going to go smoothly—it just won't. Your expectations are going to be wrong. You're going to make mistakes. Will you persevere?

Uncertainty can be the reason for tenacity, but it can also undermine it. To build tenacity—through education and training—the key is in correctly identifying, understanding, and responding to uncertainty. The problem with economics, psychology, and consequently the B-school curriculum is that they *don't* understand uncertainty correctly. Not at all.

B-schools try to teach maximization techniques based on data collection and probabilistic analysis. But that's just it—there are no probabilities in uncertainty. Such analyses get uncertainty totally wrong, so they mislead administrative business leaders.

And when things inevitably go awry for reasons that the administrative leader can't quite fathom, their tenacity becomes strained. Grit is strong when you *know* and acknowledge uncertainty, when you acknowledge the possibility of the unexpected and steel yourself for it.

When you understand the uncertainties that you face and are trained and prepared for them, they will not undermine your grit when the unexpected occurs. You'll see the island in the distance and, even though unexpected swells are pushing you around, setting your sights on this goal will help you push yourself to just keep swimming.

A BETTER WAY

Can the entrepreneurial mindset required for venture mode be taught? The answer is a resounding yes . . . *sort of*. But to do so effectively would require a radical paradigm shift in business education.

What business schools teach now isn't entrepreneurship—not really. They teach a programmatic approach to starting a business or running a development project. They teach entrepreneurship as if entrepreneurship were little different from engineering or medicine or programming—entrepreneurs just need the know-how. But that's not entrepreneurship. It's administration mode.

There's a better way. We can make business education truly entrepreneurial. We can teach an effective *venture mode* approach to entrepreneurship. And we can teach entrepreneurial leadership. But what will it take? Universities are the very embodiment of administration mode. How can they be reformed?

What's the radical solution?

CHAPTER 10

THE MBE

What's the solution to the MBA problem? It's an entrepreneurial problem with an entrepreneurial solution—or, to be more accurate, a range of entrepreneurial solutions, since there are no boundaries to entrepreneurial creativity.

In this chapter, we'll introduce our entrepreneurial solution to the supply problem of entrepreneurial leaders: an entrepreneurial alternative to the administrative education system. The range of potential solutions can extend from the incremental to the radical. Ours is in between the extremes, although it'll seem radical to most. More importantly, we're confident it can work to successfully overhaul and improve business education.

We propose two parts to our solution. The first is to build a new education system designed to instill an entrepreneurial mindset and skill set: a *master's of business enterprise* or MBE. The MBE program will be an alternative and competitor to the traditional MBA, with much broader availability.

Its programming, curriculum, and orientation will be explicitly designed to nurture entrepreneurial problem-solving and stamp out tendencies toward administrative leadership. Core to our solution are three fundamental and far-reaching innovations: (1) a new business model, (2) a new education structure, and (3) a new curriculum.

The second part of our solution is to establish a credentialing program we're calling the Entrepreneurial Leadership Institute, or ELI. The ELI will be a credentialing program aimed at expanding the training of entrepreneurial leaders. This organization would be a direct competitor to the AACSB and would accredit other entrepreneurship education programs to build, in their own way, an education system committed to instilling and nurturing entrepreneurial leadership and rejecting administration. This is an accreditation system committed to principles of innovation and entrepreneurship and the rejection of a scientific approach to management. Perhaps even established business schools who also see the problems of administration would join.

In other words, we propose to take entrepreneurship education out of the existing university accreditation system for all the reasons we've detailed throughout this book. Students trained in our MBE or a competing program credentialed by the ELI will receive a degree-quality business education and training in entrepreneurial leadership rather than administration.

THE NEW BUSINESS MODEL OF THE MBE

In venture mode, a business model is designed for and around its customers, who have important needs they would be willing to pay to have better satisfied. The entrepreneurial offering in the business model is a value proposition that demonstrably solves and satisfies the unmet need.

It's long past time to rethink the business model of higher education. Higher ed has employed the same business model and revenue structure for many generations. It's so entrenched within the institutions and culture across the globe that there have been few, if any, attempts to rethink it in modern history. But it need not continue as it always has.

The MBE, and many other educational options certified by the ELI, would be unleashed to fundamentally rethink the business model of higher education. To show that the MBE can deliver everything that's needed in business education and nothing that isn't, let's review the current university business model that we propose to replace.

THE CURRENT UNIVERSITY BUSINESS MODEL

Marc Andreessen and Ben Horowitz—partners of venture capital firm Andreessen Horowitz—outlined the purposes of the modern university very well in an episode of their *a16z* podcast,[1] distilling twelve specific purposes or jobs of the university:

1. **Credentialing:** providing students with a credential that employers use to screen candidates
2. **Education:** delivering the actual courses themselves, which purportedly provide knowledge and information that will, or may, be needed in students' future careers or lives
3. **Research production (new knowledge):** being a hybrid producer of both research and teaching (many elevate the former over the latter)
4. **Policy think tank:** designing and floating new policy ideas for government

5. **Moral instruction:** instilling values (generally, traditional values of critical thinking, open inquiry, free speech, and tolerance have given way to modern values of diversity and social justice)
6. **Social reform:** enacting social change by encouraging activism
7. **Immigration agency:** offering foreign students expedited immigration status in exchange for full tuition fees
8. **Sports league:** operating a major sports league as a huge potential source of revenue
9. **Hedge fund:** leveraging endowments and their investments, which have been key pieces of financing over the last thirty years
10. **Young adult daycare:** relieving parents of the duties of overseeing their children
11. **Dating site (and mate credentialing):** being a place where people date and choose mates (it's where Facebook originated)
12. **Lobbying firm:** directly interfacing with government on their own behalf

This list is a fascinating distillation of the modern university. University graduates will likely see the list as an accurate reflection of their own college experience. Not all of those goals matter to all students (or faculty), but all twelve of them matter to *some* of the university's stakeholders and so have been nurtured as competencies of the modern university. But as a composite of these twelve goals, universities do virtually none of them well. And some seem like they should be altogether outside of the purview of an institution of higher learning.

Indeed, we will propose that the MBE program introduced here, and other ELI-accredited organizations, focus principally, if not solely, on the two functions that matter—*education* and *credentialing*—and dispense with the rest of the list. Why? To answer the question, we must first ask, *Who is the* ***customer*** *and who should it be?*

WHO'S THE UNIVERSITY'S REAL CUSTOMER?

All venture mode innovations start by identifying the prospective customer in order to focus attention on maximizing value-creation activities for them. The prospective customer is the person or entity expectedly willing to pay for the value that's offered.

Intuitively, an answer leaps to mind: It's the *students*, right? Well, maybe. In some cases, yes. But who *really* pays the university?

If students are the customers, that would explain several of the things universities have started doing. Indeed, students-as-customers explains several items on Andreessen and Horowitz's list: (1) credentialing, (2) education, (8) sports league, and, to a lesser extent, (5) moral instruction.

If the student is a foreigner, they might value (7) immigration agency also (or primarily). And of course (11) a dating site or, perhaps more broadly, a social club. Universities have become social clubs for young adults, with many opportunities for socializing and entertainment. But, of course, what most students want most of all is a good job waiting for them at the end of their four (or more) years.

But the *customer* is defined in business model analysis as the one who pays and so is distinguished from the *consumer* or *end user* who in fact consumes the value proposition—often they're one and the same, but not always. When you buy a gift, you are the customer but not the consumer. The consumer will get some value out of consuming the gift, but it is often difficult for the customer to predict how much (which is why gift buying is so hard).

In the case of higher ed, most students don't pay tuition themselves. A 2022 survey by Barnes & Noble College Insights found that 45 percent of students were self-funding, up from 37 percent in 2019.[2] But note that the survey allowed for overlapping answers. Very few of those 45 percent *fully* paid for their college, even with student loans. Most had funding from scholarships, grants, and/or their parents. Fewer than half paid anything out of their own pocket. So it doesn't seem quite accurate to describe them as the customer.

Perhaps we might say it's the students' parents who are the real customers. If so, then this suggests a different value focus and structure for colleges. Parents-as-customers, for example, explain job item (10), young adult daycare. Parents, looking to get their child out of the house and transition them into the "real world" can put their young adult child into the care of a university and let them take over from there.

However, that same survey found only 41 percent of students report that their parents pay for college, down from 50 percent in 2019. So parents aren't the only or even primary customer either.

Maybe governments are the customer. State and federal funds amount to 38 percent for four-year universities and 58 percent for two-year schools,[3] and the Barnes & Noble College Insights study found that 51 percent of students were funded by federal monies, down from 64 percent in 2019. This suggests that the government seems to be a big customer of universities. But what do governments want? Well, they want an educated and moral populace.

So they pay for (2) education, (5) moral instruction, and (6) social reform. But most of all, governments want justification for their policies. And there are few more legitimating roles in society than academics, who are broadly held up as the "experts" in a variety of disciplines. So (4) policy think tank is the big job that garners governments' support of universities. And, of course, politicians want to be reelected, so they care about (12) lobbying also.

In the end, there's no clear customer, just a muddle. That's a fatal error in venture mode. No clear customer means no clear purpose and a convoluted organization that does none of its (twelve!) core tasks particularly well.

INNOVATING THE BUSINESS MODEL

Now let's reformulate the business model for our own aims—to develop prospective entrepreneurial leaders to start filling the high unmet demand out in the business world. To do so, we clearly want to simplify and refocus on the *actual* customer's value experience. But who are, or ought to be the real customers?

Here's one of the core insights of our MBE program—our target customer is the one stakeholder who has been almost fully neglected by modern higher ed: *employers*. Employers have the largest interest in student training as they look for employees who can join the firm and perform needed tasks effectively for the purpose of value creation and economic growth. In fact, the primary reason that college is valuable to students—the number one reason on Andreessen and Horowitz's list—is *credentialing*. That is, universities serve as a third-party verification of graduates' employability.

Why is providing a credential such a vital service? Because businesses need a way to weed out performers from nonperformers, the talented from the incapable. In other words, businesses need a way to screen prospective employees, and a college degree has traditionally been the best screening tool they've had.

In fact, this credential explains nearly the entire value-add of college. In his provocative book *The Case Against Education*, economist Bryan Caplan summarizes research on the long-term effects of higher education. There are fascinating discoveries in the literature. For example, the long-term earnings of someone who completed only three years of college are much closer to the earnings of those who had no college at all than to the earnings of those who finished their degree. If the value of college were its education, we would expect the education of three years to pay off correspondingly. But it doesn't. You have to finish to receive the credential and hence the payout.

The value of college, Caplan concludes, is not in the education that it purports to bestow (which, he shows, tends to be quite insignificant if measured as knowledge retained) but in the credential—the signal to employers that the graduate would be an intelligent and capable employee who can complete assigned tasks at a reasonably high level and is willing to obediently jump through whatever hoops are required. Students, or their parents, pay dearly for this credential in order to signal to employers that they are employable.

Fair enough. But what if there was a *better* credential—that is, better for our customer, the employer?

A college degree is a decent credential. Schools vary in their admission criteria, but university admissions essentially serve as a prescreening for employers—these are the brightest crop from high school, capable of higher-level learning and tasks. To get the absolute best and brightest, employers hire from the best universities—and pay a premium for those grads. While college graduates retain very little of their actual education, they do demonstrate in their classes a capacity to learn new information and skills and to perform assigned tasks.

While a university degree is a decent credential of overall intelligence and capacity to perform assigned tasks, it's not really enough for the purposes of the hiring firm. Employers need much more information about prospective employees to determine if they're a good *fit*. They need information about how well they work with others. They need information about their capacity to innovate and problem-solve. They need information about how they interact in real-world business situations. They need information about prospective employees' empathy, judgment, ingenuity, and tenacity.

They'd ideally like to have insight into graduates' mindset: service orientation, imagination, bias for action, systems thinking, and relentless curiosity. And they need information about their values and how they would fit within company culture.

This sort of information just isn't typically gathered by universities nor is it shared with employers. In fact, universities are incentivized to *hide* damning information about their students from employers so that their students get hired. The graduate employment rate is one of the most important selling points universities pitch to prospective students (and their parents).

Consequently, hiring is one of the most challenging aspects of doing business. A bad hire can quickly turn an organization toxic, and detoxing from the toxicity is always far more challenging and time consuming than it seems.

Picking good employees who buy into the mission, fit the culture of the organization, and contribute significant value to the organization is absolutely vital. But *how* can organizations identify those people?

Well, organizations do their best. HR does what it can to screen out the incapable. Only those who get past this initial screening, who look like they are qualified, are interviewed. The interview then serves as an extra layer of capability screening, making sure the candidate is competent and has the right skills. But it also tries to screen for cultural fit. Are they likable? Do their values align? Do they have the right mindset?

But it's not at all easy to verify application materials, and there's only so much you can learn from an hour-long interview. Candidates all put their best foot forward—even those who are mentally unstable, neurotic, sociopathic, or Machiavellian. The unscrupulous cheats generally know how to appear smart, honest, and collegial for an interview.

In short, businesses haven't been able to solve the screening problem with the existing credentials. University degrees grant employers some vantage into graduates' capabilities and work ethic but not as much as they once did. Grade inflation is real, and graduates simply aren't what they once were. It's not even their fault, really—this is the world they were given and what they were told they should do.

But universities aren't incentivized to push students, to really screen them out. They get paid to graduate students, not fail them. They're financially incentivized to churn out degrees, not screen people for the workforce.

Now is the time to totally rethink the business model of higher education.

What we're proposing is to make *employers* the paying customer.

The value proposition makes sense for them. It's clear that there is a need, since businesses are already spending a lot to recruit, onboard, and train new hires. *A lot*. Some of the costs are clear and explicit, but most are subtle and hidden—the opportunity costs of the time and effort expended by key team members who must sacrifice their productivity to find, interview, onboard, train, and mentor new hires.

HR experts estimate that the total costs of hiring a new employee can be three to four times their expected salary. "That means if you're hiring for a job that pays $60,000, you may spend $180,000 or more to fill that role," writes Katie Navarra.[4] Even then, managers often underestimate the real costs of bringing in new people. And the costs only go up if the person hired turns out to be a poor fit.

Despite its importance and the high costs of turnover, the hiring process has had remarkably few innovations. Certainly there have been some, a few of them bordering on the creepy. It's really better for *both* parties if there's a good fit, but it's more important for the employer. Bad employees can endure a job they hate if the paycheck keeps coming in. But this sort of employee can really hurt the company, reducing the productivity of all. Doing due diligence to make sure a new hire really qualifies and fits will increase the productivity of the whole team.

Business executives are all too aware of this problem. *Multiverse* reports that 67 percent of business leaders don't think the current higher education system delivers the skills needed for the workforce of tomorrow.[5] They perceive significant gaps in university business education and the resulting cost and burden on companies. Here are some specific examples from well-known leaders of the business world:[6]

> Elon Musk, CEO of Tesla, SpaceX, Neuralink, and Solar City, among others, has said in various interviews, "I think that there's too much emphasis placed on college degrees in general. The real proof of someone's ability is what they've actually done. . . . A lot of the time, we're hiring people with degrees and then having to train them from scratch anyway because what they learned in school doesn't apply directly to the real-world problems we're solving."[7]

> Jamie Dimon, CEO of JPMorgan Chase, has echoed this: "We spend a tremendous amount of time and money training new hires, even those coming out of top business schools. The gap between what's taught in universities and what we need—practical problem-solving, adaptability, and real-world financial acumen—is wider than it should be."[8]

> Satya Nadella, CEO of Microsoft, has noted their heavy investments in training: "The reality is that even with a degree, many graduates aren't ready for the pace and complexity of today's tech-driven workplace. We invest heavily in upskilling them, which shows there's a disconnect between academic preparation and the skills we need for innovation and execution."[9]

> Ginni Rometty, former CEO of IBM, noted, "Too many graduates, even from business programs, lack the hands-on skills we need—things like critical thinking under pressure or working effectively in teams. We've had to build our own training programs to bridge that gap, which is a significant cost and a sign that the education system isn't keeping up."[10]

> And Doug McMillon, CEO of Walmart, has observed, "We hire thousands of graduates every year, and while they come with theoretical knowledge, we often have to reteach them how to apply it in a practical setting. It's a burden on our resources, and it points to a flaw in how universities prepare students for the workforce."[11]

All these entrepreneurial leaders (and many more) have seen firsthand the weaknesses of the modern higher education system. It's not doing its job. Why not? Because it's deeply entrenched in administration mode. It's not customer centric. It's beyond repair. It's run by administrators for administrators, and there's little hope for entrepreneurial leadership to turn that ship around.

We need solutions from *outside* the existing administrative structure. We propose that the process of fitting employees and employers can be done by an effectively designed MBE program, which flips the business model of higher ed. Instead of students paying tuition for the education—or credential—*companies* would hire the MBE program to find, fit, and train a cohort of future employees.[12]

With paying companies as customers, rather than students, the MBE program would be refocused on the needs of the companies that are looking for new hires. The focus would be on effectively screening students for their capabilities, qualities, and values. The model would bring in students of various talents, passions, and values and nurture them, while simultaneously molding them to be a productive fit for sponsoring firms.

Note that this means that there would be, in the typical case, *no tuition cost* for MBE students. Their education would be paid for by the companies they will ultimately work for. As the nation, and the world, look at the mounting student debt problem with little hope of resolution, maybe this isn't (or shouldn't be) a political problem but an *entrepreneurial* problem. A "free to the student" MBE is quite a deal.

In terms of total cost of such training to sponsoring companies, we expect it to be significantly *less* than the total costs that those companies currently pay for hiring and training. Edie Golberg, founder of talent management and development company E. L. Golberg & Associates, estimates that the "soft costs" of productivity losses account for the bulk of an organization's total hiring costs.[13] An organization specialized in matching employers and employees for fit could reduce these "soft costs" to a minimum. There will still be some disruption, some training and mentoring, but most of the process can be done by an effective higher education organization that has hiring firms as its customers.

Perhaps more importantly, this flip of the business model would enable higher education to better train its students by tailoring the curricula to the needs of their customers—that is, the sponsoring employers. Instead of a generic education, these flipped universities would teach the most useful knowledge and skills for sponsoring organizations. It would even be possible—likely even—that sponsoring organizations could create some course content and teach courses themselves via their own training leads if they so desired.

By turning the business model toward hiring organizations, a key activity of the MBE is to match students with sponsor organizations. Here, the needs of the sponsoring organizations (the paying customers) take precedence, whereas the current student-paid tuition paradigm takes students' needs as primary.

This is important because universities' current incentives are to make their students broadly appealing to any and all organizations. But this is an inefficient model. Educational training is far too general, generic, and, to a large extent, useless. What's needed is a more selective and customized process—matching students and organizations for fit, which would allow education to be carefully targeted, curated, and tailored.

The MBE could be completed in one to two years, as we'll describe shortly. With sponsoring companies as the paying customers, the MBE would use that time as essentially a prolonged interview and internship process—similar to a residency program for medical students. Med students learn their technical knowledge in class, then their practical, experiential hours come from working as a resident. As residents, they work in real hospitals, often for long hours under high stress and emergency conditions, learning from interacting with real patients and from working with more senior doctors across a wide range of circumstances.

Whereas in business recruiting, interviews might last a day. Companies simply cannot get to know candidates as deeply as they need to in order to assess fit. Residency programs are much more successful at this and are currently perhaps the best solution available.

It may take a sponsoring organization some time to build their higher-value talent pipeline through the new MBE system. There will be a lag time between identifying prospective candidates and their graduation. In the meantime, we anticipate that sponsors will utilize the normal hiring process at the end of the funnel to meet their immediate, stop-gap hiring needs (although we might remind you that this means longer training and "upskilling" periods post-hiring).

The MBE would quickly take over, with its growing database of students and throughput of graduates who are well fitted to sponsor companies. A highly qualified talent flow would build up rapidly. All sponsor organizations would have access to the student database and would be able to fill their needs with much greater confidence. Once the MBE becomes a larger program, especially if the ELI succeeds in expanding the pool of entrepreneurship education programs, sponsor firms should be able to hire replacements from the pool of outgoing graduates easily, with much greater confidence of capability and fit compared to today's approach.

Overall, the expected consequence of this innovation to the higher ed business model is lower costs for students *and* employers, better and more tailored student training and preparation for employment, and longer-term employment with lower turnover. But can it break through the institutional staying power of the university system?

THE NEW STRUCTURE OF THE MBE PROGRAM

The second level of innovation we propose is structural. As we break out of the traditional four-year degree box, here's what such a program *could* look like.

First, the learning experience would be *tailored*. The MBE program's customer-facing team would work closely with sponsoring companies, readily sharing information with them about its students and their developing knowledge, skills, and values. In the current educational structure, students accumulate general education credits prior to tackling the requirements for their major. In our proposed new system, we replace these "general credits" with highly tuned early programming designed to develop and assess students' values and general skills in critical thinking, problem-solving, communication, and ethics.

Based on the outcomes, students will advance smoothly into technical skill development later in the program. Students would be consulted regularly and guided into a program tailored to hone their strengths and optimize their fit with one or more sponsoring organizations who have expressed interest.

Second, our new structure doesn't conform to semesters or a traditional "academic year." It's high time the semester system was reconsidered, especially in business education. Businesses don't operate in semesters, and there's no reason why business education should. Is it really the case that all subject matters are ideally taught in exactly fourteen weeks? It seems to us that the answer to this question is obviously no. But that's the way the current system is designed. Some courses cram as much material as they can in a single semester. Most, however, are forced to draw the course out with extraneous fluff.

What if we simply redesigned the curriculum structure into a *staggered* design? For instance, students could take four courses at a time, but where they are in those courses would vary. Not only is this intuitively sensible, but it would also greatly alleviate the tendency of the semester system to put students in a bind, with all of their major projects and tests due at the same time.

Perhaps more importantly, it would allow students to do more in less time. We can admit and understand that students need breaks, which the semester system facilitates. But these breaks are much longer than they need to be and cost students valuable years in the workforce.

More importantly, by moving from the fluffed semester schedule to a staggered one, we can fit a full program into just one to two years.

And a third structural innovation is the requirement of a practicum or residency. The MBE would make this practical hands-on education a fundamental part—at least half—of the MBE course. It would take the form of a supervised residency or internship, where a sponsor company assigns one or more students a real project to work on, with a real-world timetable, a real team, real goals, real budget resources—and real scrutiny. Projects could range from the technical and specific to the organizational and managerial. But in all cases, the goal of this practicum is for sponsoring organizations to bring a real problem for their prospective employees to work on.

One of the advantages of this system is that it would bring the full benefits of an internship—for both parties—into the program without (necessarily) sacrificing additional time in the program. Sponsoring organizations and students would familiarize themselves with each other in a more complete and fundamental way that allows a final and thorough assessment of fit. Misfits can be shifted quickly to other projects to minimize lost time and effort.

In this way, students find a good fit *during* their practicum, and organizations get to try out their new candidates to ensure a good fit. The practicum serves the same purpose as a residency in medical education: a bridge between medical school and full-time practice.

Another key advantage is that a sponsoring organization gets not only real, effective training but also productive work done in exchange for its sponsorship. This would go a long way toward mitigating the costs of sponsoring the MBE program. Moreover, students would gain real experience in the organization with which they are matched and, consequently, receive essential training while still in school. Upon graduation, they can hit the ground running with very little additional hiring, onboarding, or training costs.

These innovations are just a sampling of what may be possible. The goal here is not to sell a single, specific solution but instead to consider what might be possible. There has been so little innovation over the decades and even centuries that, once our minds finally break free from the paradigm of tradition, all sorts of new ideas can be unleashed.

THE MBE CURRICULUM

Finally, we need to discuss the potential innovations to the *curriculum* of the MBE. We propose a better curriculum based in *entrepreneurial* philosophy to produce true entrepreneurial employees and future leaders. We're convinced that there's tremendous, pent-up demand for precisely such employees.

Every course of business education requires a backbone of philosophy. It can't be based solely on the exigencies of the moment. Our MBE curriculum would build on entrepreneurial philosophy, which has been at the core of economics since its founding but has been eclipsed in recent times.

By way of academic background, the discipline of economics divides itself into several "schools"—you might have heard of the Keynesian school or of the Monetarist, neoclassical, or Chicago schools of economics. Entrepreneurial philosophy is a part of the foundational thinking of the *Austrian* school of economics, which is an increasingly prominent influence in the social sciences. It's saddled with this "Austrian" moniker because it originated in Vienna back when the city was one of the intellectual capitals of the Western world.

Today it's recognized in universities from the US to China—but still gets called "Austrian." We can think of it as entrepreneurial economics since entrepreneurship features so centrally in its theoretical framework. (Whereas, in the other two primary schools, the entrepreneur is wholly and conspicuously absent.) But let's stick with the "Austrian" brand name for now.

The Austrian school is a full-throated rejection of the "scientistic" administration ethos. Our proposed curriculum is designed based on this entrepreneurial economics. The following curriculum proposal is tentative, but we think it offers a useful illustration of what we think *should* be taught in a business school designed to teach an entrepreneurial mindset, a progression of entrepreneurial mindset training.

We begin with an introduction to entrepreneurial philosophy, introducing the core principles of subjectivism, intentionality, and representationalism that are foundational to entrepreneurial economics. Interestingly, these philosophical doctrines are considered heterodox in the social sciences, including economics. But they are not at all heterodox *in philosophy* at all; rather they form the "standard model."[14] In fact, it's the mainstream of economic science that adopts a heterodox (and arguably discredited) "positivist" philosophy of science.

We then introduce entrepreneurial economics in depth, along with a specific course on the entrepreneurial mindset designed to explain, motivate, and nurture a problem-solving mindset. We will also have a course on entrepreneurial ethics—the ethics of value creation. These first courses are intended to instill a specific core of understanding, mindset, and values that are at the heart of entrepreneurial leadership. They will also be used to assess the core values, beliefs, and goals of students so that we can begin to match them with aligned sponsors.

After this early stage of the curriculum, students will then turn to more practical skill development. The current proposal, as of this writing, includes in the MBE curriculum courses on design and innovation, judgment and leadership, marketing and communication, finance, accounting, macroeconomics, and strategic entrepreneurship. We also expect that sponsoring businesses will want to add specialist courses at this stage—essentially constituting "majors" or "minors" that are relevant to their industry—for their identified candidates. For example, the customer experience of supply chain management and logistics systems might be a special focus that traditional courses in those fields don't cover.

However, we must emphasize that these courses are fundamentally different from the equivalent courses at MBA programs. Our courses are premised upon entrepreneurial philosophy, whereas the courses in traditional MBA programs are derived from the positivist philosophical paradigm that is characteristic of universities' administration ethos. This isn't to say that all that is taught in such courses is bad. But entrepreneurial philosophy generates radically different conclusions in each and every subject matter, which makes our curriculum entirely unique.

The MBE will not be teaching the same curriculum as any other MBA program. Those programs are rewarded for conforming to the standards of business administration adopted by all other schools. They're all the same, much to their detriment. We do not intend to follow into such conformity. We intend to be different, to be innovative, to be entrepreneurial.

Eventually, the MBE curriculum might be expanded to offer training and development for more expansive and technical skill sets—e.g., design and engineering skill sets of various types. But all MBE students would have a foundation in entrepreneurial philosophy. We want all our students to be trained in the entrepreneurial mindset so that they can become the entrepreneurial leaders of tomorrow who will, if called upon, lead their businesses into venture mode. The MBE will become the pivot point for a shift—organizationally and culturally—from administration mode to venture mode.

THE ENTREPRENEURIAL LEADERSHIP INSTITUTE (ELI)

The MBE, as just outlined, is *our* proposed solution to the supply shortage of entrepreneurial leaders needed to keep venture mode on in modern businesses. But we're hardly so audacious as to claim that this solution, as just presented, is *the* one and only solution to the problem. Quite to the contrary, we are hopeful not to be the only intrepid venturers into this space, aiming to disrupt the higher education industry. An essential aspect of entrepreneurial leadership is to recognize that there are many creative possibilities to pursue and that the best of them will succeed if they create new value.

To facilitate such a developmental effort, legitimize such solutions, attract employers and mitigate their likely early hesitancy, and perhaps present a united front against the institutional powers that have so far impeded such innovation, we also propose the establishment of a certifying body.

Specifically, we propose the establishment of a consortium or coalition of *hiring firms* to fund and govern the establishment, development, and continuous improvement of this certifying body. This body would be charged with establishing a globally recognized professional designation in business enterprise that would assess and certify new schools committed to instilling the principles of entrepreneurial leadership.

There are many such certification bodies. A useful parallel, for example, is the CFA Institute, which oversees the chartered financial analyst, or CFA, designation. There are certification bodies in many industries. The ELI will be of this sort.

But the ELI isn't intended to be—and shouldn't become—a standard of conformity, as is the current accreditation system. Instead, it's a body that ensures commitment to an entrepreneurial philosophy, embracing in that spirit the many entrepreneurial forms that might emerge to nurture such leaders. The purpose of the ELI, then, is more than anything a signal boost of legitimacy and real commitment to entrepreneurial philosophy. The Institute would facilitate a network of aligned companies in search of entrepreneurial leaders, allowing them to turn to ELI-certified schools.

For any proposed entrepreneurial leadership education program, the certifying body would

- assess the quality of business enterprise education and mastery
- evaluate the mechanisms by which students are qualified and selected for the program
- review the nature, quality, and rigor of the curriculum
- oversee the processes of student assessment and fitting
- liaise with participating employer firms to supervise the process of the residency (the component of the ELI in which candidates work for sponsoring firms on an internship for both practical work experience and audition for fit with a hiring firm's culture)
- provide continuing professional development for a culture of lifelong learning

The board of governors would be drawn from the consortium of sponsoring businesses who fund the ELI body. In this way, hiring firms' guidance for both standards and content would be provided directly. The sponsors would staff, direct special development projects, inject content, and generally supervise the program to produce the best business-qualified graduates to meet employer needs.

Change is difficult. It's risky. Hiring MBEs might sound great in principle, but at least at the outset, because of the uncertainty that exists in any entrepreneurial undertaking, the credential is just as risky, or more so, as hiring MBAs.

Initially, we expect only those firms who are the most frustrated with modern MBA graduates—i.e., those with the greatest unmet need—to take the entrepreneurial leap with us to the MBE. But by establishing a recognized and distinguished credentialing body, we hope to alleviate employers' hesitancies and allow the MBE and MBE-like programs to grow and expand.

Eventually, we foresee the MBE sweeping the world. Will there still be a place for traditional universities? For MBAs? Probably. The world needs some administrators. But the glut of them isn't sustainable, and the global economy seems to be pining for MBEs. But as they're actively being disrupted, it seems likely that some business schools would pursue ELI credentialing. We would welcome it. It's time for the world to change.

CREATING VALUE LONG TERM

The core thesis of this book has been that businesses, in order to continue creating value over the long term, must stay in *venture mode*. Never turn it off. Never make the switch to administration mode. Your value proposition *must* change. It must improve and keep improving, sometimes radically so. Businesses haven't "made it" once their market has been validated and it's time to scale. Yes, scaling is difficult. We get why it seems right to turn to experienced administrators to do it. But businesses who do must proceed with great caution, never fully turning the reins over to administrators. That will lead to stagnation and, ultimately, to failure.

To keep venture mode on requires perennial entrepreneurial leadership. It always has. For a long time, the errors of administrative leadership were masked by the slow rates of change in the economics and competitive structure of world industries. For a long time, business leaders could win by running a tight ship because the ships were always moving so slowly.

But that just doesn't work today. Ships have changed—they're much faster now and keep getting faster. The rate of change in the world has accelerated beyond the capacity of administration mode to cope. If you run a tight ship in administration mode, you're running it into the ground.

It's the Red Queen effect. In Lewis Carroll's fable *Through the Looking Glass*, he tells the story of when Alice met the Red Queen:

> Just at this moment, somehow or other, they began to run. Alice never could quite make out, in thinking it over afterwards, how it was that they began: all she remembers is, that they were running hand in hand, and the Queen went so fast that it was all she could do to keep up with her: and still the Queen kept crying "Faster! Faster!" but Alice felt she could not go faster, though she had not breath left to say so.
>
> The most curious part of the thing was, that the trees and the other things round them never changed their places at all: however fast they went, they never seemed to pass anything. "I wonder if all the things move along with us?" thought poor puzzled Alice. And the Queen seemed to guess her thoughts, for she cried, "Faster! Don't try to talk!"
>
> Not that Alice had any idea of doing *that*. She felt as if she would never be able to talk again, she was getting so much out of breath; and still the Queen cried, "Faster! Faster!" and dragged her along. "Are we nearly there?" Alice managed to pant out at last.
>
> "Nearly there!" the Queen repeated. "Why, we passed it ten minutes ago! Faster!" And they ran on for a time in silence, with the wind whistling in Alice's ears, almost blowing her hair off her head she fancied.
>
> "Now! Now!" cried the Queen. "Faster! Faster!" And they went so fast that at last they seemed to skim through the air, hardly touching the ground with their feet, till

suddenly, just as Alice was getting quite exhausted, they stopped, and she found herself sitting on the ground, breathless and giddy.

The Queen propped her up against a tree, and said, kindly, "You may rest a little now."

Alice looked round her in great surprise. "Why, I do believe we've been under this tree the whole time! Everything's just as it was!"

"Of course it is," said the Queen, "What would you have it?"

"Well, in our country," said Alice, still panting a little, "you'd generally get to somewhere else—if you ran very fast for a long time, as we've been doing."

"A slow sort of country!" said the Queen. "Now, here, you see, it takes all the running you can do, to keep in the same place. If you want to get somewhere else, you must run at least twice as fast as that!"[15]

BUSINESS TODAY NEEDS VENTURE MODE

Business operates the Red Queen's way. It's not enough to run at pace. You must constantly be getting *faster*, so to speak, creating *more* value.

Today businesses need organizational agility. They need to be innovative. They need creativity. They must beat their competitors not by being more efficient than them but by finding ways to create more value than they do for more people. Today's markets are too dynamic to rely on efficiency for competitive advantage. New value is created too quickly. And if a business isn't the one creating the new value, it's the one being disrupted.

To train entrepreneurial leaders who can lead such agile organizations and persistently out-innovate the competition, we need to totally rethink education. That has been our goal for the past couple of years. The result of our work is the MBE.

But this is just the beginning. We sincerely believe the MBE and the Entrepreneurial Leadership Institute are the future of business education. There will be immense institutional resistance from the universities, of course. Investing in and starting the MBE, being one of the first sponsors or students—all of this will involve taking some potentially big risks. We look forward to collaborating with businesses and students who, like us, believe that the MBA is ripe for some creative destruction.

CONCLUSION

The engine of economic growth is *entrepreneurship*—the fountain of new value creation. The world would be a better, more thriving environment if every business operated in venture mode, aiming single-mindedly at creating new value for both customers and colleagues and earning the market's reward in return. There'd be much more productivity, more wealth created for all, and far less bureaucratic waste.

What's stopping us?

Administration.

We're entraining our youth into an administration mindset. They go on to be hired by our businesses, entrenching successive cohorts of administrators, generation after generation. These administrators become managers and then executives who run their businesses in administration mode.

We propose to educate new cohorts of entrepreneurial venturers who can spread their creative influence throughout the economy. This will require taking business education out of the university and totally rethinking it.

Our proposal for a master's of business enterprise (MBE) is a radical alternative—a totally new approach to education—that will entrain an entrepreneurial mindset. At long last, we can start to balance the supply of entrepreneurial leaders and administrators, limited only by the market—how many MBE grads will firms want to hire and how many individuals want to qualify for those jobs. We can end the artificial scarcity of entrepreneurs.

In fact, the MBE can be expanded in response to market need. It can be layered for higher and higher levels of specialization (e.g., targeted to financial markets or digital engineering), and it can be extended across demographic groups (e.g., junior MBEs for high school students).

The Entrepreneurial Leadership Institute (ELI) will facilitate this expansion with not only our MBE but also various others' innovative solutions.

The ultimate goal is to turn all jobs and roles on the production side of the economy into value-creation jobs. At the same time and as a consequence, we can eliminate administrative waste. We can bypass the unnecessary overhead of bureaucracy, relieve the sclerosis of compliance, and release the creativity of the individuals we've condemned to serve in these roles.

For over a century, businesses have become increasingly focused on administration. They do so in an attempt to control and smooth outcomes because financial markets insist on predictability and avoiding surprises. Venture mode doesn't aim for predictability. It aims for breakthroughs. It doesn't call for control. It calls for imagination, creativity, and experimentation.

We believe that the opportunity would be best seized by establishing a consortium of business firms who see a pathway to recruiting and developing a group of venturers to strengthen their human capital for the never-ending pursuit of new value.

James Dyson, chairman of the iconic manufacturer Dyson, told the *Wall Street Journal* in an April 2025 interview that his company doesn't hire university graduates, preferring to run its own internal company university. Not every company has the bandwidth for such an investment. For those companies, we offer our unique MBE formula of in-person education, online active learning, rigorous exams, and a "practicum" (i.e., residency) to demonstrate capability, application, and cultural fit.

It's time to rethink how we find and train new hires for the innovative businesses of the modern age. For those who would like to join us in this development, please contact us.

APPENDIX A

OUTLINE OF COURSES FOR THE MBE

The following represents a summary of the learning content in an MBE curriculum. The outline will be enriched by the latest interactive online technologies and designs, AI tutors, practice with tools and techniques, cohort-based online and in-person discussions and seminars, interactions with business executives and entrepreneurs, and the "practicum" of the internship or residency with one of the sponsoring businesses.

COURSE NAME	DESCRIPTION
Introduction to Entrepreneurial Economics	This foundational course would cover the basic principles of entrepreneurial economics, including subjective value, marginal value, the customer's value learning cycle, the role of entrepreneurship, and relevant parts of the theories of money and capital.
Philosophy and Economics: Why Economics Matters	This course would provide grounding in the philosophical and ethical context for value creation, entrepreneurship, and business.
Entrepreneurial Economics and Business Strategy: Economics Applied to Business	This course would explore how entrepreneurial economic theories can inform business strategy, including pricing, production, design, marketing, innovation, capital combination and recombination, and organizational/ corporate structure decisions.

COURSE NAME	DESCRIPTION
Entrepreneurship	This course would delve into the role of entrepreneurship in a business framework, at every scale and stage. It would examine the entrepreneurial discovery of important needs and the pursuit of implementation opportunities through resource allocation and market processes.
Ethics, Value Creation, and Entrepreneurial Economics: Morality in Business	This course would explore how entrepreneurial economics relate to business ethics and value creation, helping students make ethically sound business decisions that create value for consumers and customers, ultimately leading to value for stakeholders and shareholders. Win/win (markets) vs. zero sum (politics) has a moral component.
Global Economics and Policy: The Distinctive Perspective of Entrepreneurial Economics	This course would explore global economic systems, monetary policy, and governmental actions (especially regulation) from an entrepreneurial economics perspective.

COURSE NAME	DESCRIPTION
Innovation, Disruption, and Growth: A Continuous Process	This course would use Schumpeter's concept of "creative destruction" (equivalent to disruption in modern business terminology) as context for business development and growth, with a special emphasis on the role of innovation and technological change and would view the market as a process: unpredictable and unknowable.
Design Process: Value as a Customer Experience	This course would design backward from the customer experience and examine the role of entrepreneurship in bringing innovation to market via empathic diagnosis of customer needs and dissatisfactions translated through a design process into new value propositions.
Marketing	This course would demonstrate the fundamental role of marketing for bringing customer understanding and a customer needs diagnosis into the firm as a feedback loop and communicating and delivering new value propositions back to the customer.

COURSE NAME	DESCRIPTION
Interdisciplinary Studies in Entrepreneurial Economics	This course would help students integrate their understanding of entrepreneurial economics with other business disciplines like finance, management, marketing, and strategy.
Advanced Seminar in Entrepreneurial Economics	This course would be a discussion-based seminar examining advanced topics in entrepreneurial economics and their application to contemporary business problems.
Entrepreneurial Economics and Financial Management: Debt, Equity, and Financial Decision-Making	This course would focus on the principles of financial decision-making, the role of interest rates, and the structure of capital from an entrepreneurial economics perspective.
Finance and Accounting	This course would demonstrate the application of finance and accounting as a means to further entrepreneurial ends, using the two kinds of accounting: managerial and financial.

COURSE NAME	DESCRIPTION
Communication for Entrepreneurs	This course would equip students with skills to effectively communicate complex economic theories to diverse audiences in business and policy contexts.
An Entrepreneurial Economics Approach to Understand Money and Interest Rates	This course would provide an in-depth understanding of business cycle theory, monetary policy, and macroeconomic stability from an entrepreneurial viewpoint.
Practicum	This course would require students to apply their knowledge of and learning in entrepreneurial economics to a practical business project, demonstrating their mastery of the subject and their ability to make sound business decisions, work collaboratively in teams, and fit into a corporate culture while actively creating value for customers.

APPENDIX B

CURRICULUM FOR THE MBE

Curriculum design is driven by learning objectives, including these:

- **Understand the core principles of entrepreneurial economics,** such as subjective value, the market process, uncertainty, emergence, and economic calculation, and how they facilitate innovation.
- **Apply entrepreneurial economic thinking to decision-making processes,** including capital allocation, product pricing, marketing strategy, and managing entrepreneurial risks, in businesses at every stage and of every size.
- **Recognize the role of knowledge and knowledge building,** with knowledge as the critical entrepreneurial resource and knowledge building as continuous improvement and the route to advantage.

- **Apply systems thinking and economic problem-solving** by understanding the principles of complex adaptive systems and the role of constraints and context, developing critical thinking skills necessary to analyze and interpret economic events, and creatively applying these insights to solve real-world business problems.
- **Explore entrepreneurial value creation** by understanding the central role of entrepreneurship in the economy and in business, including entrepreneurs' role in exploring and exploiting new value opportunities, coordinating resources, and driving market processes.
- **Examine empathic value creation and ethical decision-making** through learning the role of empathy in the creation of business strategies that facilitate value for their customers and stakeholders, guided by ethical considerations and the long-term sustainability of their business operations.
- **Understand experience design** and work backward from imagined experiences to prototypes and testing.
- **Build foundational knowledge of global economic systems and policy**, including the role of monetary policy and the impact of governmental regulatory actions on business cycles, within the context of Austrian economic thought.
- **Master the principles of marketing,** including its primary function in the development of customer understanding and how it nurtures and monitors feedback loops, disseminates customer knowledge to all functions of the firm, and frames and presents new value propositions to customers.

- **Apply value-creating innovation to business strategy and development** and appreciate the role of innovation and technological change in value creation.
- **Explore principles of organizational design**, emphasizing structures that unleash autonomous creative potential as opposed to control through authority relations.
- **Build interdisciplinary understanding** though integrating economic understanding with other business disciplines such as management, finance, marketing, and strategy to facilitate holistic business decision-making.
- **Develop strong communication skills** to effectively convey and advocate for Austrian economic principles in diverse business and policy contexts.

NOTES

PREFACE

1 J. W. Dawson, & J. J. Seater, "Federal regulation and aggregate economic growth," *Journal of Economic Growth*, 18, (2013): 137–177.
2 Ibid., p. 138.
3 R. Bailey, "Federal Regulations Have Made You 75 Percent Poorer," Reason, June 21, 2013, https://reason.com/2013/06/21/federal-regulations-have-made-you-75-per/.
4 J. B. Bailey & D. W. Thomas, "Regulating away competition: The effect of regulation on entrepreneurship and employment," *Journal of Regulatory Economics*, 52 (2017): 248.
5 P. L. Bylund, *The Seen, the Unseen, and the Unrealized: How Regulations Affect Our Everyday Lives* (Lexington Books, 2016).

CHAPTER 1

1 Thank heavens for tenure!
2 Amy Hughes, "How Many Forbes Billionaires Have MBAs?," Businessbecause.com; March 12, 2020, https://www.businessbecause.com/news/in-the-news/5260/how-many-forbes-billionaires-have-mbas.
3 Bryan Caplan, *The Case against Education: Why the Education System Is a Waste of Time and Money* (Princeton University Press, 2018).

4 We arrive at this rough estimate from multiple studies, several of which we'll introduce later in this chapter, that show a clear performance advantage by founder-led companies that align with what we refer to as "venture mode." Our task, of course, will be to demonstrate that the reason that founders outperform MBA-led firms is they don't suffer from the administrative mindset instilled in MBA programs.

5 Frederick W. Taylor is regarded as the "father" of scientific management, the application of nineteenth-century scientific principles to the practice of management, captured in his book, *The Principles of Scientific Management*. It was published in 1909 and voted the most influential management book of the entire twentieth century by the Fellows of The Academy of Management.

6 Gallup reports that global employee engagement declined to 21% in 2024, https://gallup.com/workplace.

7 Paul Graham, "Founder Mode," PaulGraham.com, https://www.paulgraham.com/foundermode.html.

8 Vicky McKeever, "iPod inventor Tony Fadell: 'I literally had a decade of failure,'" CNBC, June 10, 2020, https://www.cnbc.com/2020/06/10/ipod-inventor-tony-fadell-i-literally-had-a-decade-of-failure.html.

9 Tony Fadell, The Verge interview, 2016.

10 https://venturebeat.com/games/zynga-history/.

11 Ibid.

12 Lerong He, "Do founders matter? A study of executive compensation, governance structure and firm performance," *Journal of Business Venturing*, 23(3) (2008): 257.

13 R Fahlenbrach, "Founder-CEOs, investment decisions, and stock market performance," *Journal of Financial and Quantitative Analysis*, 44(2), (2009): 439–466.

14 C. Zook & J. Allen, The founder's mentality: how to overcome the predictable crises of growth (Harvard Business Review Press, 2016).

15 P. Murugaboopathy & G. Dogra, "Founder-led firms outpacing CEO-led ones in market recovery," Reuters, 2020, https://www.reuters.com/article/global-companies-founders-idUSKBN2741U5/.

16 H. Terbeck, V. Rieger, N. Van Quaquebeke, & A. Engelen, "Once a founder, always a founder? The role of external former founders in corporate boards," *Journal of Management Studies*, 59(5) (2022): 1284–1314.

17 https://www.paulgraham.com/foundermode.html.

18 Chesky admits as much in a follow-up interview: https://www.theverge.com/24279570/airbnb-ceo-brian-chesky-founder-mode-apple-steve-jobs-management-decoder-podcast-2024.

19 To be more precise, value is better understood not as being "created" but as being facilitated by the entrepreneur. But that's an argument for another day. See Mark's other book, *Entrepreneurial Valuation*, to go down that rabbit hole.

CHAPTER 2

1 https://www.theverge.com/24279570/airbnb-ceo-brian-chesky-founder-mode-apple-steve-jobs-management-decoder-podcast-2024.
2 Graham's blog post reported on Chesky's presentation, but Chesky clarified that Graham was the one who in fact coined the terms "founder mode" and "manager mode."
3 https://www.paulgraham.com/foundermode.html.
4 https://finance.yahoo.com/news/steve-jobs-adopted-no-bozos-130000529.html.
5 https://www.theverge.com/24279570/airbnb-ceo-brian-chesky-founder-mode-apple-steve-jobs-management-decoder-podcast-2024.
6 https://www.paulgraham.com/foundermode.html.
7 https://www.inc.com/marcel-schwantes/a-young-steve-jobs-once-gave-this-priceless-leadership-lesson-here-it-is-in-a-few-sentences.html.
8 https://www.theverge.com/24279570/airbnb-ceo-brian-chesky-founder-mode-apple-steve-jobs-management-decoder-podcast-2024.
9 https://spectrum.ieee.org/xerox-parc.
10 ARPA was the US military's Advanced Research Projects Agency and developed many computer technologies, including ARPANET, arguably the first modern computer network using the TCP/IP protocol.
11 https://spectrum.ieee.org/xerox-parc.
12 Ibid.
13 Ibid.
14 Ibid.
15 https://theworldofcomputingcomp1220uwi.weebly.com/adele-goldberg.html.
16 https://d3.harvard.edu/platform-rctom/submission/eastman-kodak-from-market-leader-to-bankruptcy.
17 H. C. Lucas Jr, & J. M. Goh, "Disruptive technology: How Kodak missed the digital photography revolution," *The Journal of Strategic Information Systems*, 18(1) (2009): 46–55.
18 Ibid.
19 https://www.nbcnews.com/id/wbna7813791.
20 Ibid.
21 https://www.fool.com/investing/general/2011/12/09/the-worst-ceos-of-2011-part-1.aspx.

22 H. C. Lucas Jr, & J. M. Goh, "Disruptive technology: How Kodak missed the digital photography revolution." *The Journal of Strategic Information Systems*, 18(1) (2009): 51.
23 https://money.cnn.com/2009/10/21/autos/auto_bailout_rattner_excerpt.fortune.
24 http://s.wsj.net/public/resources/documents/BA_gm_memo.pdf.
25 https://www.nytimes.com/2009/11/13/business/13auto.html.
26 https://money.cnn.com/2009/10/21/autos/auto_bailout_rattner_excerpt.fortune.

CHAPTER 3

1 According to the National Center for Educational Statistics, there are about 200,000 MBA graduates in the US annually. Another estimated 400,000–600,000 graduates are generated annually outside the US.
2 Internal email to Tesla staff quoted in Inc., Oct 30, 2017: "An Email from Elon Musk Reveals Why Managers Are Always a Bad Idea."
3 https://plato.stanford.edu/entries/dilthey/.
4 https://plato.stanford.edu/entries/brentano/.
5 Saint-Simon employed a young Auguste Comte as an aide, and they worked together to develop positivism. After Saint-Simon's death, Comte proved to be the true mind behind positivism. But Comte and Saint-Simon did not see eye-to-eye on the philosophy. Comte was, in fact, quite impressed and influenced by French Ideology, whereas Saint-Simon was contemptuous of the bourgeois liberal Ideologues. Saint-Simon's influence was significant throughout the nineteenth century, but Comte's work has had a much more lasting impact on the philosophy of science.
6 It's a topic for another day, but this positivist philosophy is the root of the eugenicist movement that was quite popular in the early twentieth century across the developed world.
7 H. A. Simon, *Models of My Life* (MIT Press, 1996), 75.
8 A. Camuffo, A. Cordova, A. Gambardella, & C. Spina, "A scientific approach to entrepreneurial decision making: Evidence from a randomized control trial. *Management Science*, 66(2) (2020): 564–586.
9 T. Zellweger, & T. Zenger, "Entrepreneurs as scientists: A pragmatist approach to producing value out of uncertainty," *Academy of Management Review*, 48(3) (2023): 379–408.
10 R. E. Rose, & C. Wong, "The MBA and corporate leadership: If a CEO of a large corporation has a graduate degrees, it likely is an MBA," *Business Horizons*, 32(5) (1989): p. 54.

11 D. Rasmussen & H. Li, "The MBA Myth and the Cult Of the CEO," Institutional Investor, February 27, 2019. https://www.institutionalinvestor.com/article/2bswcr8vbel8iskltcq2o/corner-office/the-mba-myth-and-the-cult-of-the-ceo.
12 https://www.institutionalinvestor.com/article/2bswcr8vbel8iskltcq2o/corner-office/the-mba-myth-and-the-cult-of-the-ceo.
13 https://preply.com/en/blog/best-college-to-become-a-ceo/.
14 https://www.washingtonpost.com/business/2018/10/22/more-top-performing-ceos-now-have-engineering-degrees-than-mbas/.
15 A. Gottesman & M. R. Morey, "Does a better education make for better managers? An empirical examination of CEO educational quality and firm performance," An Empirical Examination of CEO Educational Quality and Firm Performance (April 21, 2006). Pace University Finance Research Paper (2004/03), (2006).
16 S. Bhagat, B. J. Bolton, & A. Subramanian, "CEO education, CEO turnover, and firm performance," Available at SSRN 1670219 (2010).
17 G. Zandi, S. Y. P. Lok, A. Aslam, & D. Singh, "Is a MBA degree necessary to Be a CEO of large corporation: the case of fortune magazine global top 100 corporations?," *International Business Research*, 8(12) (2015): 102.
18 https://www.institutionalinvestor.com/article/2bswcr8vbel8iskltcq2o/corner-office/the-mba-myth-and-the-cult-of-the-ceo.
19 D. Miller & X. Xu, "A fleeting glory: Self-serving behavior among celebrated MBA CEOs," *Journal of Management Inquiry*, 25(3) (2016): 286–300.
20 D. Miller & X. Xu, "MBA CEOs, short-term management and performance," *Journal of Business Ethics*, 154 (2019): 285.
21 https://mintzberg.org/blog/mbas-as-ceos.
22 T. King, A. Srivastav, & J. Williams, "What's in an education? Implications of CEO education for bank performance," *Journal of Corporate Finance*, 37 (2016): 287–308.
23 https://www.cnbc.com/2018/12/05/worlds-oldest-billionaire-yun-chung-chang-goes-to-work-every-day.html.

CHAPTER 4

1 Airbnb CEO Brian Chesky on what 'founder mode' really means | The Verge.
2 Frederick W. Taylor, *The Principles of Scientific Management*, Introduction (Harper, 1911), 6.
3 Fraser Institute, https://www.fraserinstitute.org (Olson, 2013).
4 Fraser Institute: Economic Freedom of the World 2024, https://www.fraserinstitute.org/categories/economic-freedom-world.

5 Index of Economic Freedom, Heritage Foundation, 2024.

6 R. Holcombe, *Entrepreneurship and Economic Progress* (Routledge, 2007).

7 P. G. Klein, M.D. Packard, & K. Schnatterly, "Collaborating for innovation: The role of organizational complementarities," in Reuer, J. J., Matuskid, S., & Jones, J. (eds.) *Oxford Handbook of Entrepreneurship and Collaboration* (Oxford University Press, 2019).

8 https://hbr.org/2017/04/how-self-managed-teams-can-resolve-conflict.

9 Marc Andreessen interviewed by Chris Williamson: The Truth About Elon Musk; 2024 https://www.youtube.com/watch?v=FQ4wBv0w9ew.

10 Doug Kirkpatrick, *Beyond Empowerment: The Age of The Self-Managed Organization* (Business Agility Institute, 2017).

11 R. M. Kanter & N. H. Dai, "Haier: Incubating entrepreneurs in a Chinese giant," Harvard Business School Case, 2, 318 (2018), https://hbsp.harvard.edu/product/318104-PDF-ENG.

12 M. J. Greeven, K Xin, and G. S. Yip, "How Chinese Companies Are Reinventing Management," *Harvard Business Review* (2023).

13 Handu's Journey to Success; whoknowschina.com/case-study; 2024.

CHAPTER 5

1 https://www.amazon.jobs/content/en/our-workplace/leadership-principles, 1996-2025.

2 J. Stiglitz, "The ultimate goal of any economy is to increase the well-being of its citizens," www.project-syndicate.org/commentary/after-neoliberalism-progressive-capitalism-by-joseph-e-stiglitz-2019-05.

3 SuiteFeedback blog, June 2019, Amazon and Customer Experience

4 M. Packard, "Entrepreneurship: toward the Nirvana state of rest," *MISES: Interdisciplinary Journal of Philosophy, Law and Economics*, 7(3) (2019).

5 M. Brenan, "U.S. Confidence in Institutions Mostly Flat, but Police Up," Gallup, July 15, 2024, https://news.gallup.com/poll/647303/confidence-institutions-mostly-flat-police.aspx.

6 https://www.theverge.com/24279570/airbnb-ceo-brian-chesky-founder-mode-apple-steve-jobs-management-decoder-podcast-2024.

7 Gary Hamel and Michele Zanini, *Humanocracy: Creating Organizations As Amazing As The People Inside Them* (HBR Press, 2020).

8 A. Thierer, Permissionless innovation: The continuing case for comprehensive technological freedom (Mercatus Center at George Mason University, 2016).

9 W. J. O'Donnell, MD, "Reducing Administrative Harm in Medicine–Clinicians and Administrators Together," *The New England Journal Of Medicine*, June 22, 2022.

10 Michele Zanini, "The Accountability Dodge," Substack, May 6, 2025.

11 "Zappos Culture Of Delivering Happiness," digitopia.co, October 2024.

12 "Why Dyson Founder Says He Has Lived a Life Of Failure," *Wall Street Journal*, April 26, 2025.

CHAPTER 6

1 Richard Rumelt, *Good Strategy, Bad Strategy* (Penguin Random House, 2011).

2 For full disclosure, Mark hates the SWOT analysis tool so much he won't let his students use it.

3 J. B. Barney, "Strategic factor markets: Expectations, luck, and business strategy," *Management Science*, 32(10) (1986): 1231–1241.

4 J. Barney, "Firm resources and sustained competitive advantage," *Journal of Management*, 17(1) (1991): 99–120.

5 To be fair to Mr. Olsen, he claims to have been referring to the bulky system that he and his competitors designed, not personal computers, which were still yet to hit the scene. But that's kind of the point. So many failed to see the future of computing, including Xerox executives.

6 A job to be done is defined as a "circumstances-based description of understanding your customers' desires, competitive set, anxieties, habits, and timeline of purchase," https://online.hbs.edu/blog/post/jobs-to-be-done-framework.

7 https://www.youtube.com/watch?v=BpXtAhiKHBE.

8 Erik Larson, "How Jeff Bezos Uses Faster, Better Decisions To Keep Amazon Innovating," *Forbes*, 2018.

9 James Currier, "70 Percent Of Value In Tech is Driven By Network Effects," nfx.com, 2019.

10 https://x.com/fowltown/status/1124056098925944832

11 R. Hastie, "Problems for judgment and decision making," *Annual Review of Psychology*, 52(1) (2001): 655.

12 See "On the roles of function and selection in evolving systems," Michael L. Wong et al, PNAS Research Article September 10, 2023.

13 John H Miller, *A Crude Look At The Whole* (Basic Books, 2015).

14 https://kaizen.com/what-is-kaizen/. Kaizen is a philosophy of continuous improvement that encourages employees (without specific top-down direction) at all vertical levels and horizontally across departments to entrepreneurially make small, incremental changes to improve efficiency and quality and reduce waste.

CHAPTER 7

1 https://theresanaiforthat.com/.
2 Ben Cohen, "It's Waymo's World. We're all just riding in it," *Wall Street Journal*, wsj.com May 30, 2025.

CHAPTER 8

1 https://www.pbs.org/nerds/part3.html.
2 Musk has diagnosed himself with Asperger's. Asperger's, as a diagnosis, has largely fallen out of favor in the medical industry because it references a specific position, or range, of the autism spectrum toward the end of higher functionality. It is, thus, not its own unique diagnosis but merely a variant of a wide range of autism spectrum disorder.
3 W. Isaacson, *Elon Musk* (Simon and Schuster, 2023).
4 https://www.businessinsider.com/elizabeth-holmes-theranos-steve-jobs-obsession-2018-5.
5 If this sounds like a reproach of you as a business leader, we have high hopes for you!
6 https://gutmann-archived.president.upenn.edu/meet-president/what-makes-university-education-worthwhile.
7 Ibid.
8 In a 2025 report, Paul Wiltshire claims that "as university participation began to rise above 30 per cent of the young-adult population around two decades ago, the graduate premium disappeared to an average of zero for the extra graduates in the higher education system." Source: https://www.telegraph.co.uk/news/2025/05/31/public-misled-value-university-degree-statistics-debt-loans/.
9 https://bellwether.org/wp-content/uploads/2024/04/DollarsAndDegrees_1_Bellwether_April2024.pdf.
10 If this sounds like sour grapes, we can assure you that Mark is quite well published. He's fortunately in a field where debate is still widely accepted and appreciated.
11 J. Haidt, The Righteous Mind: Why Good People Are Divided by Politics and Religion (Vintage, 2012).
12 https://www.ed.gov/laws-and-policy/higher-education-laws-and-policy/college-accreditation.
13 https://www.ed.gov/laws-and-policy/higher-education-laws-and-policy/college-accreditation/accreditation-in-the-us.
14 R. Koppl, *Expert Failure* (Cambridge University Press, 2018).
15 https://www.aacsb.edu/about-us.
16 https://www.aacsb.edu/educators/accreditation/business-accreditation.

17 https://www.aacsb.edu/-/media/documents/accreditation/aacsb-global-standard-setting-framework.pdf.
18 https://thielfellowship.org/.
19 Ibid.

CHAPTER 9

1 https://www.wsj.com/articles/SB10001424052970204603004577267271656000782.
2 Noam Wasserman was a Harvard Business School professor at the time (in 2012) and is now the dean of the Sy Syms School of Business at Yeshiva University.
3 Founder and CEO of Right To Start, a nationwide campaign to expand entrepreneurial opportunity for all.
4 https://www.wsj.com/articles/SB10001424052970204603004577267271656000782.
5 https://www.inc.com/tim-askew/why-entrepreneurship-cant-be-taught.html.
6 H. Zhao, S. E. Seibert, & G. T. Lumpkin, "The relationship of personality to entrepreneurial intentions and performance: A meta-analytic review," *Journal of Management*, 36(2) (2010): 392.
7 B. Hogendoorn, I. Rud, W. Groot, & H. Maassen van den Brink, "The effects of human capital interventions on entrepreneurial performance in industrialized countries," *Journal of Economic Surveys*, 33(3), (2019): 798.
8 https://www.wsj.com/articles/SB10001424052970204603004577267271656000782.
9 F. V. Hayek, "Scientism and the study of society. Part I." *Economica*, 9(35) (1942): 267–291.
10 T. Felin, A. Gambardella, E. Novelli, & T. Zenger, "A scientific method for startups," Journal of Management, 50(8), (2024): 3080–3104.
11 T. Zellweger & T. Zenger, "Entrepreneurs as scientists: A pragmatist approach to producing value out of uncertainty," *Academy of Management Review*, 48(3) (2023): 379–408.
12 R. McBride, M. D. Packard, & B. B. Clark, "Rogue entrepreneurship," *Entrepreneurship Theory and Practice*, 48(1) (2024): 392–417.
13 The $4 price tag of the Pet Rock in 1975 amounts to over $20 today.
14 L. La Bella, *Steve Jobs and Steve Wozniak* (Rosen, 2016): 79.
15 https://www.startups.com/articles/can-entrepreneurship-be-taught.
16 N. Berg & G. Gigerenzer, "As-if behavioral economics: Neoclassical economics in disguise?" *History of Economic Ideas: XVIII*, 1, 2010 (2010): 1000–1033.

17 F. V. Hayek, "Scientism and the study of society. Part I," *Economica*, 9(35) (1942): 267–291.
18 L. v. Mises, Human Action, Scholar's Edition, p. 13. (Ludwig von Mises Institute, 1998).
19 W. Gates, *Business @ the Speed of Thought* (Penguin, 2000): 208–209.
20 To learn more about this, see Mark's previous book, *Entrepreneurial Valuation: An Entrepreneur's Guide to Getting Into the Minds of Consumers.*
21 W. Chan Kim and Rene Mauborgne, "Blue Ocean Strategy: How To Create Uncontested Market Space And Make The Competition IIrrelevant" (Harvard Business Review Press, 2014).
22 The first scholarly mention of this term that we could find appears in D. G. Reinertsen & P. G. Smith, "The strategist's role in shortening product development," *The Journal of Business Strategy*, 12(4) (1991): 20. It has since been repeated frequently.
23 A. Dietrich & R. Kanso "A review of EEG, ERP, and neuroimaging studies of creativity and insight," *Psychological Bulletin*, 136(5) (2010) p. 822.
24 A. l. Duckworth, C. Peterson, M. D. Matthews, & D. R. Kelly, "Grit: perseverance and passion for long-term goals," *Journal of Personality and Social Psychology*, 92(6) (2007): 1087.
25 D. De Clercq & I. Belausteguigoitia, "The usefulness of tenacity in spurring problem-focused voice: The moderating roles of workplace adversity," *Journal of Business and Psychology*, 32 (2017): 480.
26 I. Santos, V. Petroska-Beska, P. Carneiro, L. Eskreis-Winkler, A. M. M. Boudet, I. Berniell, . . . & A. L. Duckworth, Can grit be taught? Lessons from a nationwide field experiment with middle-school students (No. 15588), IZA Discussion Papers, (2022).
27 F. H. Knight, *Risk, Uncertainty and Profit* (Houghton Mifflin, 1921).

CHAPTER 10

1 https://a16z.com/podcast/crisis-in-higher-ed-why-universities-still-matter-with-marc-ben/.
2 https://www.prnewswire.com/news-releases/college-students-are-contributing-more-to-their-higher-education-costs-survey-finds-301526431.html.
3 https://bellwether.org/wp-content/uploads/2024/04/DollarsAndDegrees_1_Bellwether_April2024.pdf.
4 https://www.shrm.org/topics-tools/news/talent-acquisition/real-costs-recruitment.

5 PR Newswire, June 6, 2023, https://www.prnewswire.com/news-releases/67-of-business-leaders-dont-think-the-current-higher-education-system-delivers-the-skills-needed-for-the-workforce-of-tomorrow-301842538.html.

6 All these composite quotes are distilled from actual discussions and annual reports using Grok 3.

7 Commentary from various interviews, including his critique of traditional education systems in favor of practical skills.

8 Paraphrased from discussions on workforce readiness in annual shareholder letters and interviews.

9 Adapted from remarks on workforce development and education in speeches and Microsoft's talent strategy discussions.

10 Drawn from her comments on IBM's P-TECH initiative and critiques of traditional education.

11 Paraphrased from discussions on Walmart's workforce training investments and retail industry challenges.

12 Clayton Christensen's "jobs to be done" theory posits that customers "hire" products or services to fulfill specific tasks or achieve desired outcomes in their lives rather than purchasing them for their features alone. "Know Your Customers' 'Jobs To Be Done,'" *Harvard Business Review*, 2016.

13 Ibid.

14 B. Epstein, *The Ant Trap: Rebuilding the Foundations of the Social Sciences* (Oxford University Press, 2015).

15 Lewis Carroll, *Through the Looking Glass* (Harper & Brothers, 1902): 36–38.

ABOUT THE AUTHORS

Hunter is a lifelong practitioner of venture mode. He was educated in England before that country adopted the MBA, so he escaped with a master's degree in economics. It wasn't until his professional career, however, that he learned the core practice of venture mode and brand building and established a global consulting practice to apply its principles across multiple companies, industries, and countries, with outstanding results.

He's been a Silicon Valley start-up CEO and a general partner in a seed-stage venture capital fund, where administration counts for nothing and agility in understanding customers and markets and designing and innovating new value propositions at speed count for everything. Hunter's experience-based knowledge provides the deep, venture-industry perspective that practical business professionals expect of an author.

Mark is a tenured professor of management with academic expertise in entrepreneurship theory. Yes, he sometimes teaches in his school's (executive) MBA program. This gives him an important insider's perspective into the system and curriculum—what is being taught and how—and its flaws.

As a researcher, he's published over forty peer-reviewed scholarly papers on entrepreneurship theory, the philosophy of science, and entrepreneurial economics, which are all featured in the book's arguments. Mark's academic work provides the core theoretical foundation for our case. Yes, in a way, he's biting the hand that feeds. Fortunately, his current employer has been all too happy to let him teach venture mode and entrepreneurial leadership to his students.

We're convinced the thesis of this book is a paradigm-breaking argument. We hope you'll come away from it likewise convinced that you need to turn venture mode on—and keep it on.